I *CAN* SPEAK

*Conquering fear and building confidence
in high-stakes speaking situations.*

Dr. M. Paula Daoust

BehaviorTransitions.com

I *Can* Speak: Conquering fear and building confidence in high-stakes speaking situations.

Dr. M. Paula Daoust

Copyright © 2020 Maplewheat Publishing
Cover design by Germancreative

Co-editors: Pamela Brisendine and Dorissa Daoust

First Printing: December 2020

ISBN-13: 978-1-7353697-2-3

Dr. M. Paula Daoust
Behavior Transitions

10940 Parallel Pkwy., Suite K-182,

Kansas City, KS 66620
(785) 633-6078

www.BehaviorTransitions.com

www.ICanSpeakbook.com

Dr. M. Paula Daoust is available to speak at your business or conference event on a variety of topics. Call (785) 633-6078 for booking information.

Why Read This Book

When you must speak in front of others, do you notice your hands getting a little sweaty or is your stomach feeling queasy? Are you short of breath or is your heart beating faster? These are normal responses to situations such as a job interview, giving a speech or an important presentation or proposal, toasting the bride, being called upon in a meeting or talking to strangers at a networking function. All these situations have one thing in common; the perception that you are being judged. That makes the stakes high and stress is a natural outcome.

If, however, the stress response becomes overwhelming, it can be a problem for both your career and your sense of self-esteem. If your response to a high-stakes speaking situation is to avoid it altogether, or when it can't be avoided, you find yourself freezing up and unable to find the right words, it's time to do something about it. And this is just the right book for you!

Imagine how your life would be different if you confidently embraced high-stakes speaking situations. How would your career improve if you could be calm and think clearly in these situations? With the tools in this book, you can discover for yourself how calm and confident you can be in any high-stakes speaking situation.

Are you ready to make a lasting change?

This book can be your guide to showing up in high-stakes speaking situations with confidence and clear thinking. You can mix and match the practical tools included according to your own comfort and style. You can prove to yourself that you can be calm when you need it most.

Additional free resource material for this book is available at:

https://www.ICanSpeakbook/Resources

Written by a Leading Expert with 30 Years' Experience

Dr. M. Paula Daoust has a doctorate in Behavior Psychology and is an expert in helping people find and maintain their peak performance. She is also a certified hypnotherapist and seamlessly blends these tools into her coaching to help people easily achieve lasting change. Over 25 years, she has taught hundreds of master-level students how to be more persuasive and influential, and how to successfully manage conflict.

Dr. M. Paula Daoust is the expert other leaders look to for help in finding their peak performance. She has taught workshops and spoken at events all over North America on subjects such as conflict, change management, storytelling, influence and power, anxiety and stress at work, and peak performance.

Do you want Dr. M. Paula Daoust to be the motivational speaker at your next event?

Call (785) 633-6078

or visit

www.BehaviorTransitions.com

Table of Contents

1
Introduction

Do the butterflies take flight in your stomach at the thought of delivering a presentation, going to a job interview, or being called to answer in an important meeting? These are challenging situations that can leave you feeling stressed and looking for a way out if you are like many of us. But, it doesn't have to be like that. When you are confronted with situations in which all eyes are on you, you can feel confident and calm, and you can think and speak clearly.

I can remember when my eighth-grade teacher announced that everyone would write and deliver a five-minute speech. The three best speeches would then have the honor of competing with the other classes during the next school assembly which would include the entire student body, all the faculty and many parents. At recess, my best friend, Ellie, told me she was going to be selected for the competition and not only that, she was going to win. Although I say we were best friends, in reality we were rivals, always working to out-do the other. So, I had no choice but to throw myself into this challenge. I wasn't about to let Ellie walk away with this achievement, uncontested.

I worked hard at preparing my speech and did a pretty good job. As a result, despite my butterflies, I was selected to compete in the assembly. However, to my frustration Ellie was also chosen to compete, and I knew she didn't write her speech. Her older sister had written it for her! Ellie had cheated on this assignment. It irritated me to no end that she would have the same opportunity to compete at the school event.

Regardless, I practiced my speech and made four little cue cards. I underlined key words and memorized my lines. I was ready for the big day. When it was my turn to speak, I strode onto that stage and looked out at the audience. I had never done anything like this before and now I was staring at over 100 people in a cramped auditorium. All eyes were on me. The lights felt hot and I felt my temperature rise. The butterflies in my stomach had become bumble bees and they were stinging. I swallowed hard and began speaking. I was about half-way through my speech when, horror-struck, I realized that my cue cards had somehow gotten out of order. I was lost. I tried to gather myself and find the right card but then my knees began to shake. I thought I was going to fall over the edge of the stage and right into my teacher's lap. I did the only thing that I could think to do at that moment: I ran off stage. Have you ever had an experience like this? Perhaps you didn't run away, but you wished you could?

Later, after all the speeches were done, I sat on the edge of the stage, swinging my legs and hoping that, somehow, the judges would overlook the fact that I didn't finish my speech. Perhaps they would see what a great job I had done up until that fateful moment. Of course, they didn't. And to make things even worse, Ellie won the contest. In my heart, I firmly believed that if I had finished that speech, I would have won. That day, I made up my mind that I would never run off a stage again and, more importantly, I would become a great speaker. Or, at the very least, I would become comfortable speaking in situations in which the stakes were high and all eyes were on me.

Speaking in the spotlight can translate to different situations, but they all have one thing in common. You might be giving a presentation, called on to answer a question in a meeting, anticipating a job interview, talking to an authority figure, or raising a controversial issue to a group. Perhaps you have even found yourself alone at a networking event. There is a common denominator that makes them all difficult. In each of these situations, all eyes are on you. You believe, whether it is true or not, that you are being judged. In all these situations and any other similar context in which all eyes are on you, your fight-or-flight response is in full force. Thinking clearly can become a challenge.

After years of practice and paying attention to what helped and didn't help, I have developed tools that can make a difference for you. Recently I spoke to an audience of over 500 people. I would be lying if I told you that I didn't feel any tension or anxiety, but it was at a level that helped me be more mindful of my presentation details. I was able to focus on serving my audience. I didn't have any butterflies although I did pass on eating any of the food they had offered the attendees. My hands were dry and my knees were steady. I felt in control. I believed in the content of my presentation, and I was excited at the opportunity to share it with those good folks.

The difference between this event and my eighth-grade experience is that I learned how to prepare my emotions and thoughts. I used the tools I will share with you in this book, and because I did that, I had an enjoyable experience. And, based on the feedback from my audience, they did too!

Being comfortable speaking in situations in which the stakes are high is the key to accelerating your career and achieving almost any goal. When you are calm rather than frantic, you will think more clearly, and you can articulate your ideas more precisely. Since most people are uneasy when speaking in a spotlight context, when you improve your comfort with speaking in such situations, you differentiate yourself from the crowd. All things being equal, you will get that job you want, influence your team to accept your ideas, and be regarded as a leader who can get things done. How nice would it be to feel enthusiasm and excitement at the opportunity to speak to a group instead of feeling dread and fear as the date approaches?

When you read the following chapters and practice the tools described, I promise that when you are faced with a high-stakes speaking situation, you will feel confident, calm, and able to both think and articulate your ideas clearly. Not every tool will be right for you but there will be tools that make a significant difference for you within the following chapters. It is time for you to break free from unnecessary constraints and have the future you deserve.

2
What's Going On?

"My manager wants me to apply for the team-lead position in her department," Rene said in a distraught tone.

"That's a compliment, but you sure don't look happy about it," I responded.

"Well, I'm kind of bored with my current position. I think I would enjoy the challenge of working with others one-to-one and helping them get better at their work. Besides, it's a promotion and I could really use the extra money. But the thought of going through a job interview, and then, if I get the job, the weekly update reports I would have to make in front of the management team, scares me to death. I don't want to disappoint my manager by not applying, but I get sick to my stomach just thinking about it."

"Oh, my, you're between a rock and a hard place! Can you tell me more about what happens to you when you think about the job interview or those presentations to the management team?" I asked.

Rene looked distressed. "I feel like I'm going to vomit. I start to feel hot and I think I'm going to pass out. My mind freezes up and I just can't think. When they ask me questions in the interview, I'm going to look so stupid, like I don't know what I'm doing."

"There's a part of you that must want to apply, or you wouldn't have stopped by to see me," I pointed out. "You got *this* job, so you know you can be successful in an interview."

"Kelly interviewed me for this job, and it wasn't really a formal interview. We already knew each other from a previous employer and she just checked in with me to see if I wanted the job. She was desperate to get someone in the door, and she knew I could do the work. It isn't the same situation as this team-lead position at all."

"What bothers you the most?" I asked. "Is it the job interview or having to make frequent presentations to management?"

"Both! And I will have to lead meetings with my team. That makes me just as nervous," Rene responded.

7

Your body and high-stakes speaking

Have you ever felt like Rene? Have you let opportunities slip past you because you couldn't muster the courage to step into the spotlight, to speak when the stakes were high? If you have experienced something like Rene's response when you anticipate speaking in front of others, you are not alone. Most people dread these kinds of situations.

When all eyes are on you, your mind is registering "threat." As a species, we do not have the defense of crushing jaws, fierce claws, speed, or a poisonous bite. Our survival depends on being a member of a pack that cooperates and supports its members. When you are the center of attention, whether it is real or just your perception, others are judging your performance as acceptable or unacceptable.

We don't live in a world that exposes us to the real danger of lions, tigers, and bears, but the evolution of our brains has not kept up with the very fast changes that have occurred in our living environments. Our brains are wired in pretty much the same way as the brains of our ancient ancestors. The potential for being found wanting or not acceptable represents rejection by the pack and leaves you vulnerable to the dangers of the wild.

When you are feeling the threat of rejection, and again, that threat could be real or just your perception, your body is going into fight-or-flight mode. That means blood, and with it the very important oxygen supply, is being diverted from your brain to give your muscles and internal organs the energy needed to run away or defend yourself. Your heart starts beating faster, your breathing becomes shallow, and your muscles tense up. Only enough oxygen is left in the brain to maintain essential functions such as keeping your heart beating and your lungs breathing. Since your brain needs oxygen to think and, with less oxygen available, it is not processing thought as much and more behavior is being controlled on auto-drive. The quality of your thinking has literally become "dumbed-down."

As part of the fight-or-flight response, your body is also flooding your body with cortisol. This is a good thing when you are facing the very real threat of being devoured by a lion, tiger, or bear because it makes you hypervigilant to subtle changes in your environment. It takes several hours for the cortisol to dissipate and this allows you to maintain vigilance well after the threat has passed, ensuring that you will be alerted quickly if the threat re-emerges. The problem with this is that cortisol also interferes with the optimal functioning of the hippocampus. The hippocampus is where working memory resides and learning occurs. It is also responsible for turning off the fight-or-flight response. When cortisol is overwhelming the hippocampus, brain neurons are being killed off faster than they can be replaced. The result is that you cannot do your best thinking and, worse, your ability to shut down the alarm system has been eroded.

With all of this going on, it's no wonder we dread high-stakes speaking! It's important to understand that there are four aspects to this response. The first thing you notice is the physical changes in your body. The list of changes is extensive and different people will experience a different combination. A few of the most common changes include stomach upset, a faster heartbeat, sweating, and dry mouth. Your thinking becomes distorted and thoughts of failure and rejection dominate. Your body seems to take on a mind of its own, and you find yourself pacing, your knees shaking, or you wring your hands. Finally, your mood has shifted to fear and distress. None of this is fun.

It can't be ignored

We are wired to pursue pleasure and avoid unpleasant events. When we engage in pleasant activities or avoid unpleasant activities, our brain rewards us with a variety of feel-good chemicals which includes dopamine, oxytocin, serotonin, and endorphins. When we are under threat, the feel-good chemicals are nudged out by cortisol. What this means is that our bodies will reward us if we avoid situations that prompt our fight-or-flight response. The problem is, the more you avoid a situation that makes you uneasy, the stronger your fear grows. The situation is controlling you because you have altered your behavior to avoid it. This leaves you with an experience of failure. Each time you avoid the situation, the sense of failure is added to previous feelings of failure, and the distress becomes greater and greater. It also begins to generalize to other situations. You might have started out fearing a presentation, but as times goes by, you find yourself avoiding speaking at a team meeting or skipping networking events.

Figure 1: Anxiety / Avoidance Curve

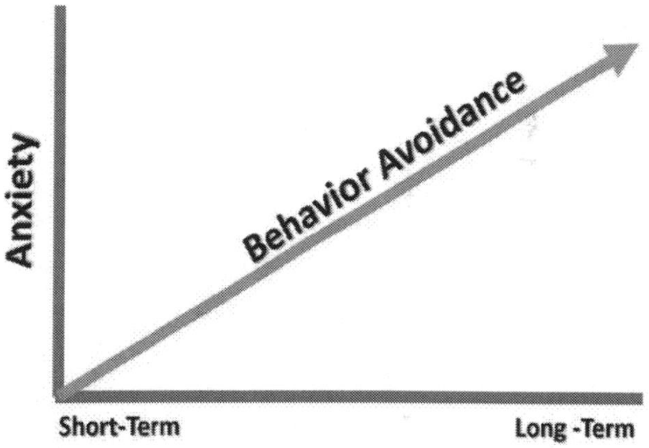

Stress can be your ally

You make your sense of failure worse when you tell yourself you shouldn't feel stressed. What you say to yourself matters and being hard on yourself because your body is responding the way it was designed to respond is futile and counter-productive. It's time to get out of your own way. You can do that by changing how you think about your stress response. Instead of telling yourself that you shouldn't feel stressed, you can embrace the stress as your friend and ally.

Figure 2: Yerkes-Dodson Law: Anxiety-Performance Curve

In 1908, Robert Yerkes and John Dodson demonstrated that some level of arousal or stress is needed for optimal performance, but also that there is a limit. Once arousal or stress goes beyond a certain point, performance deteriorates. This has become known as the "Yerkes-Dodson Law," and it is highly relevant to high-stakes speaking. When you are anticipating a speaking event in which all eyes are on you, if you don't feel any stress, you will be complacent about your preparation. The result will be a sloppy or poor performance. As your level of stress rises, you enter the eustress zone; it is in this zone that optimal performance resides.

Eustress, a term coined by Hans Selye in 1974, is the positive stress we all need. Eu comes from the Greek prefix "good" and was used to distinguish this type of stress from distress. As Selye noted, not all stress has the same effect on the body. You will feel distressed when your resources are outstripped by the demands you are facing. When this happens, you will feel as if you do not have control and the fight-or-flight response will be in full force. Distress wears you down and leaves you vulnerable to a variety of physical ailments, negative emotions, and deteriorating self-esteem and self-efficacy.

However, when *eustress* is present, the challenges you are facing are slightly out of your comfort zone but still achievable. This experience is beneficial because it fosters a sense of fulfillment and positive feelings. It increases your focus and concentration and it creates a sense of inspiration, autonomy, and resilience.

Rather than seeing stress as the enemy, you can begin to view it as your friend. You don't want to escape from stress. Rather, you want to activate it while putting some practices in place to keep it from going past eustress to distress. Up until now, your physical responses to a high-stake speaking situation has probably been interpreted as a bad thing. You can now reconsider this thinking and replace it with the knowledge that, if managed well, your stress response can be your friend. It will help you to put your best foot forward so that you can represent yourself well. Eustress will push you to prepare well and help you to think more clearly once you are speaking.

3

What Bothers You the Most?

"Ugh, I have to give my report to the VPs tomorrow. I'm not going to be able to sleep tonight," Brice said as he entered the room.

"Why won't you be able to sleep?" Willis asked curiously.

Bryce responded, "Just thinking about that presentation makes my entire body tense. In bed tonight, I know I'm going to go over my speech a thousand times. When I have to do this sort of thing, it's like my head is stuck in high gear. It's the only thing I can think about. I just hope that I don't choke tomorrow."

"I get that," Willis agreed. "I'm okay with presentations, but job interviews get to me. I can't believe they hired me for this job. I didn't think I answered their questions very well and I was sweating like crazy!"

Different contexts for high-stakes speaking

There are many contexts in which you might feel that when all eyes are on you, whether it is true or not, you are being judged. In these situations, your performance will often have an impact on your future and for that reason you want to perform at your best. Often, however, it feels as if your body is conspiring against you.

You might begin by feeling some level of distress in just one of these contexts. However, over time, if you have been avoiding situations like these, you might make an unpleasant discovery. The angst you felt in the first context has now generalized to include other high-stakes speaking contexts. For example, instead of just feeling anxious about platform speaking, you might start feeling anxious about social events. As discussed in the previous chapter, the more you avoid a situation that makes you uncomfortable, the more uncomfortable it becomes. It's like spilled syrup that you don't clean up — it simply spreads and becomes a sticky mess.

Which of the following creates a sense of anxiety for you? Score yourself on each of the following:

0 = Completely comfortable; 1 = Minor uneasiness; 3 = Some tension; 4 = Growing anxiety; 5 = High anxiety.

☐ *Platform speaking:*

This is the term used for presentations in which you are speaking for an extended period of time to inform others about something. It is an original, factual speech that has usually been prepared in advance and might have visuals such as slides to support the content. This is the context that tends to bother more people and be the most anxiety-producing.

☐ *Social events:*

This is similar to platform speaking in that it tends to be unidirectional. You are speaking to an audience about something, but this time, the setting is less formal and probably includes food and/or alcohol. You might have a relationship with many of the people in your audience. This context includes wedding toasts, eulogies, and impromptu comments at supper or lunch events. The speech tends to be shorter and might or might not be prepared in advance. Visuals such as slides or short videos can be used but more often they are not included. Even though these speeches tend to be much shorter than a platform speech, they produce almost as much anxiety for most people.

☐ *Job interviews:*

While you might like being invited to a job interview because it means a new opportunity is available, few people enjoy the actual interview. You anticipate what the interviewer might ask and worry about what you will wear. You stress about how you can best impress a stranger or strangers and convince them that you are the right person for the job. It's a lot to handle for anyone. This can, and does, create enough angst to influence us to stay in jobs we don't like, jobs that are not challenging to us, or jobs that keep us in an emotionally toxic environment.

☐ *Reporting:*

Sometimes we need to give a verbal report on the progress of a project, make a proposal, or share data on an issue. This presents a dual challenge. Not only are you worried about how you come across, but you might also be concerned about how your report will be viewed. Will members of the group accept your analysis, question your data sources, or ask you questions you hadn't considered? Verbal reports are usually to a smaller group. You might have prepared your comments in advance or you might choose to simply walk your way through the report. A written report may have even been submitted in advance and the report is just a verbal question and answer session.

☐ *Small Groups:*

This context most commonly occurs in team meetings or informal gatherings in which a decision is needed. Contributing your thoughts to issues facing the group opens you up for questions and potential criticism. If there is more than one person involved in setting a direction, there will almost always be more than one idea about how best to proceed. This is fertile ground for conflict and even if it is mild conflict, it can be enough to encourage a person to keep their thoughts to themselves.

☐ *Training:*

Corporate training relies heavily on peer-to-peer learning. This means that participants in a workshop are often asked to provide their perspective of a concept or to demonstrate the application of a new tool. This can feel risky. Others might not agree with your perspective or think your response is too shallow, etc. When you demonstrate a new behavior taught in the class, it is likely you won't do it perfectly because it is new to you. The potential for being judged negatively in this situation is very real.

☐ *Authority:*

Most people have been socialized to respect people in authority. We tend to see them as somehow different from ourselves. They are wiser, stronger, more knowledgeable, etc. It's hard enough to initiate a conversation with a stranger but when this stranger is perceived as having the power to influence your future, it is even more difficult.

☐ *Networking events:*

Almost every conference has an opportunity to meet and greet other attendees. Check out any career advice book and you'll notice that the value of creating a personal network of associates is extolled time after time. So, given the potential value of networking, why do so many people hate doing it? It's likely something to do with the unpredictability of the situation and the many unknowns it present. What do you talk about? Will you accidentally offend another person? Will your conversation sound mundane or worse, stupid? What is the other person's motivation for talking to you? Do they just want something from you? Are they really interested in you or are they just filling in time? Where do I put my hands when I'm talking? Will I spill food or my drink when I am talking? These are just a sample of the questions that might go through your mind before a networking event. If you are plagued with any of these or similar questions, your anxiety is building. Before you know it, simply skipping the networking event seems like a pretty good option.

What's your score?

How many of the different speaking contexts did you score three or higher? These are the contexts that you will want to address. The following chapters contain great strategies for managing your stress response when dealing with a situation in which you are speaking and the stakes are high. You can treat them like a buffet. Pick and choose and combine strategies according to what feels right for you. Practice them and you will do better. Remember, you don't want to eliminate the stress response. First, that might not be possible. Second, doing so will move you too far in the wrong direction and will create a new set of problems. You just want to dial your stress back from distress to eustress and that is very possible with practice.

Notice that I said you need to practice twice. I can give you a $5,000 bike, but unless you train, you will not win any races. The right equipment, tools, or strategies are part of your success; however, these things will never eliminate the need for training.

This brings us to an important point: How will you know for sure that you are making progress? You need a baseline that you can use to compare your progress. Unfortunately, your memory of what it feels like now will not be a reliable measurement. You need something a little more objective. I have provided a handy assessment tool, the *High-Stakes Speaking Scale* for this at www.ICanspeakbook.com.

You can take the assessment today and then, after you have practiced your chosen mix of strategies for three months, you can return and retake the assessment. I promise you, if you are diligent about using the tools in the following chapter, your score will improve. Take a few minutes now to see where you stand on the High-Stakes Speaking Scale. Be sure to print your results and put them in a safe place so that you can compare your results later.

4
Breathe Right

In chapters five through ten, I will present a variety of tools each of which has the power to control your stress response. You can use any combination of these tools and you will change your stress response from distress to eustress. I strongly encourage you to pick and choose among these alternatives. However, there is one tool that you will need to use with all these strategies. To be fully effective, you need to learn to *breathe*.

Yes, you have been breathing all your life but there are different ways of breathing. The words *inspiration* and *respiration* have the same Latin root *spir,* which means "to breathe." Your normal pattern of breathing tends to be at the top of your lungs. Take a minute and, without changing anything, notice your breathing. If you are raising your shoulders and chest, you are not breathing in a way that will help you with stress. If you breathe right, you can create a calm mind, have more focus, develop clearer thinking and, gain energy.

When you are stressed, you adopt the worst possible breathing pattern of short and rapid breaths, instead of your normal, light breathing. This short and rapid pattern is ideal if you are running away from a tiger. It signals the brain that there is a threat in the environment. In response, your brain activates the sympathetic nervous system to begin pumping adrenaline and cortisol into your bloodstream. All non-essential functions are put on hold and energy is diverted to the muscles and internal organs to facilitate speed in escaping the threat or strength to fight the threat off. All thought processes are running on automatic.

This short and rapid breathing is not very helpful when all you need is to answer a few questions about the report you submitted or to remember the words of your prepared presentation. In high-stakes situations, you don't need to run away or physically fight anything, but your body is responding as if you do need to run or fight. Given the challenge that you are facing, the sympathetic nervous system response is the opposite response to what you need. Instead, what you do need is calm, clear thinking so that you can complete your task with maximum efficiency, insight, and accuracy.

Fortunately, the parasympathetic nervous system can rescue you. When you breathe deeply, completely filling your lungs, you activate this alternative system. When the parasympathetic nervous system, also known as the *rest and digest system*, is turned on, your heart rate slows down, your blood pressure is lowered and your mind calms down. You are taking in more oxygen which is the fuel your brain needs for complex processing. The result is the calm and clear thinking that will contribute to feeling more confident and in control.

The key to activating the parasympathetic system is to breathe deeply, mindfully pushing the air deeply into your lungs. You fill up your diaphragm with fresh air, and then you exhale deeply, thereby flushing all the carbon dioxide out. It's the carbon dioxide in your system that contributes to feelings of light-headedness, weakness, tingling, and feeling faint. The more it builds up in your body, the more anxious and jittery you feel. By inhaling deeply and exhaling fully, you counter the sympathetic nervous system's impact, and you can take control of your thinking and your emotions. You might say the diaphragm is the "king" of confidence.

There are two techniques that you can use to calm yourself when you are feeling anxious. The first technique I will describe goes by different names: abdominal breathing, belly breathing, or deep breathing. I prefer to call it "beach ball breathing" because the visual can help us master the process. The second technique is one I prefer because it forces me to be focused on my breathing. As much as I love it, I prefer to do it in private, so I am somewhat restricted in its use. The second technique is called "alternating nostril breathing." I will describe both techniques and suggest that you experiment with them both.

Beach ball breathing

1. Put yourself in a comfortable position, sitting or lying down. Uncross your legs or arms and unclasp your hands. As you breathe in oxygen, you want that wonderful energy to be unrestricted as it moves through your body, feeding your muscles, tissues, fibers, and cells in your body.

2. Place one hand on your abdomen, just below your ribcage and the other on your chest. As you get better at this you won't need to place your hands this way. For now, they offer you feedback as you practice.

3. As you breathe in, keep your head level and do not raise your shoulders. The purpose of the hand on your chest is to provide a signal to you in case you raise your shoulders. Count to four as you inhale. As you bring in air, imagine you have a beach ball just below your ribs and you are filling it with the air you are breathing in. Push the air down into that beach ball and feel it

expand with your other hand. Your stomach should be pushing your hand out.

4. Count to five as you exhale. Pull all the air out of the beach ball, leaving it deflated. Your hand will gently drift back to its original position. It is important to breathe out at least one count longer than your breath in. When you do this, it will stimulate your vagus nerve, which in turn will signal your body to relax.

Repeat this beach ball exercise at least three times before beginning any of the strategies in the coming chapters.

Alternating nostril breathing

1. Just as with beach ball breathing, you will want to place yourself in a comfortable position. Be sure that both your arms and legs are uncrossed and resting in a relaxed manner, and that you are in a place where it is unlikely you will be disturbed.

2. Place your right-hand thumb against the right side of your nose.

3. Use just enough pressure to close your nostril.

4. Inhale through your left nostril and then, with your left-hand thumb, close that nostril.

5. Release the pressure on the right nostril and exhale deeply.

6. With the left nostril still closed, inhale deeply through the right nostril.

7. With your right-hand thumb, close your right nostril and release the pressure on your left nostril.

8. Exhale completely through your left nostril.

9. This process is one cycle. Repeat steps two through eight at least three times prior to engaging in a high-stakes speaking situation.

The power of the breath

There is a reason people tell you to breathe when they see you are tense or upset. It's because breathing alone, if done correctly, is calming. All meditations and mindfulness exercises and many hypnotic inductions use focused breathing as part of their procedures. By focusing on your breath, you give your conscious mind something to do. When you are counting your breaths, you are not thinking about whatever it is that is causing you stress. When your mind wanders back to the anxious thought, which it will, you can gently return your attention to your breathing. Using focused breathing, you are giving yourself a much needed mental break.

Adding focused breathing to any of the other tools described in the following chapters makes them so much more effective. It will put your mind in the right frame to maximize the effects of any tool. If you get nothing else out of this book, at the very least learn to use beach ball breathing or alternating nostril breathing. If you do, these tools alone will make spotlight speaking easier. But why settle for easier? Use any combination of the following tools, and anxiety about speaking in high-stakes situations will be in your past. You will be free to perform at your best.

5

What You Say to Yourself Matters

Aaron explained proudly, "I'm really hard on myself. I set high standards and expect to meet them."

"And what does that mean when you don't measure up?" I asked.

"I get really down on myself. I push myself even harder because I expect more from myself," he admitted.

Getting out of your own way

In some ways, I agree with Aaron. It is important to set goals and push yourself out of your comfort zone. Stretching to achieve something difficult is the way you

29

grow. Setting a standard for yourself or others is a way of saying, "I believe in you - I believe that you have more in you, and that with effort, you can be more than you are right now." That is a sincere compliment, and when you do achieve the difficult goal or meet that higher standard, it feeds your self-esteem. So far, so good.

The problem comes when you are not able to achieve the goal or meet the standard or when either the goal or the standard was too big a stretch. If you can realistically assess the situation and either adjust your expectations or accept that it was the goal or the standard and not you that failed, it can be a learning experience. No harm, no foul. However, that isn't what Aaron did. Maybe you are like Aaron and instead of letting it go, you become extremely self-critical.

When folks like Aaron come to me for help, I ask them to share with me precisely what they say to themselves. I am often saddened by what I hear. The things they say to themselves - and maybe the things you say to yourself in similar situations - are nothing short of mean, bullying, harassing, aggressive, and sometimes even tormenting. If anyone else said those things to you, it would be considered verbal abuse.

Why do people talk to themselves like this? One answer is that they think if they punish themselves, it will motivate them in the future and lead to better results. Another answer is that, since we are wired to seek pleasure and avoid unpleasant events, heaping punishment on a failure will make the failure so unpleasant that we will avoid challenging ourselves in the future. In effect, the negative self-talk is a message to our subconscious not to step out of our comfort zone. It serves as a reminder that we are not good enough. If we already know that we will fail, then why even try?

The downward spiral to defeat

In chapter two, I described what happens in your body when you become anxious. It is the same sequence when you speak negatively to yourself. It follows this path:

- You set a goal or set an expectation of meeting a certain standard on a project.

- You work toward that goal, but something gets in the way, or the goal or expectation was unreasonable, and it appears that you won't get the results you wanted. Or, you don't get the results you wanted.

- Now, you start criticizing yourself.

- This negative self-talk sets off negative feelings such as anger, frustration, shame, and sadness.

- These negative feelings warn the subconscious that the world is not safe, and your body then activates the fight-or-flight stress response.

- Blood rushes away from your brain to provide energy to fight or run, leaving you less energy to process thoughts.

- Cortisol floods your body, hampering your hippocampus from doing its work. Your ability to turn off the stress response is now challenged, and learning is also compromised.

In this condition, you cannot possibly do your best. You are literally not firing on all cylinders. The result is that this negative self-talk makes it harder to achieve your goal or meet the standard for yourself. You are getting in your own way. Your negative thinking is now serving as a self-fulfilling prophecy because if, in the future you think about setting a goal or you set an expectation for yourself, the memory of this failure will come rushing back.

Figure 3: Self-talk

Downward Spiral Of What You Say To Yourself

With the memory of failure comes the negative feelings and self-criticism, "I won't succeed. I never succeed. I'm not good enough. I'm not smart enough." Your self-criticism is likely to be a little different than the few examples written here, but it probably has the same flavor. This self-criticism now ensures that you will not be able to bring your best self to the task. The result is predictable: you won't achieve the goal or meet the standard the way you wanted to. And now you have one additional example of failure to feed those negative thoughts.

Stinkin' thinkin'

Stuart Smiley, a character on *Saturday Night Live* in the late 90s, referred to self-criticism as *"stinkin' thinkin'"* and I can't think of a better description. This pattern of self-punishment when we don't achieve the goals or standards, we set for ourselves achieves nothing. Brené Brown, in her book *"I Thought It Was Just Me"*, refers to the negative response as shaming, and she argues that this pattern is an epidemic. The issue with shame is that no one talks about it, so, as she points out, we all think we are the only ones who experience shame. Some folks are just better at faking it than others. Does it help you to know that you are not alone, that just about every person you interact with is suffering from some shame?

This brings us to another very important concept: the imposter syndrome. It is surprising just how many high-achieving, successful folks walk around wondering when they are going to be found out as imposters or fakers. Despite their success, they don't believe they are as smart, talented, or athletic as others perceive them to be.

I first noticed this when I was studying for my doctorate. I was certainly guilty of this kind of thinking and when I talked to my fellow students about their brilliant work, they too felt that someone was going to call their bluff, and they would be exposed as imposters.

This is stinkin' thinkin', and for me, it meant that I undervalued my research and never published it. This kind of thinking results in dismissing opportunities or not even seeing them in the first place. It doesn't have to be this way. You can break free of this cycle. It begins with replacing these unhelpful thoughts with energizing, hopeful thoughts.

Self-affirmations

A self-affirmation is simply a statement you make to yourself that recognizes your value and worthiness. It is a tool for counter-balancing the waves of negativity you inflict on yourself. A self-affirmation provides your subconscious with a different and more helpful direction to focus its effort. Your subconscious will work on any outcome you set for it, so why not give it a more constructive outcome to work toward?

A successful outcome depends as much on your attitude toward your goal or personal standard as your effort. Epictetus, the great stoic philosopher, once said, "It's not what happens to you, it's how you react to it that matters." You expected and wanted oranges but got lemons instead. If you see the lemons as a bad thing, then you have a sour piece of fruit for your snack. If, instead, you see the lemons as an opportunity to make lemonade, you now have something to enjoy.

Applying this to high-stakes speaking situations, if you see them as scary and dangerous, failure and embarrassment are not far behind. Race car drivers understand that the car goes where the eyes are focused. If they see the wall and not the small sliver of space between them and the other car, then they are going to hit the wall. When you respond to situations in which you feel that being in the spotlight is a bad thing, it's going to be a bad thing. Without consciously doing so, you will engage in thoughts and subtle behaviors that make failure inevitable. Being calm and confident in these situations begins with deliberately and methodically practicing a different response. Remember Henry Ford's warning, "If you think you can or can't, you're right."

Writing a self-affirmation

Returning to Stuart Smiley, he is famous for his affirmation, "I'm good enough. I'm smart enough. And doggone it, people like me." This isn't a bad self-affirmation statement but a better one is Emile Coué's iconic mantra, "Every day, in every way, I'm getting better and better." This is a powerful affirmation because it is optimistic, it suggests movement toward change, and you are not claiming to be something your subconscious knows you are not.

For a self-affirmation to be effective in counter-balancing your negative thinking, it must be a statement that is not only positive, but your subconscious must also be able to act on it. To do that, your subconscious must accept it. You can't trick your subconscious into believing the sky is green if your eyes are registering blue. If you want to be wealthy, then telling yourself, "I live in a mansion," is not going to move you toward your goal if in reality you are living in a 500-square-foot tiny house.

You can't lie to your subconscious. It just doesn't work that way. What you can do is change that self-affirmation slightly to, "I am doing all the things I need to do so I can I live in a mansion." Now you're cooking with gas! Your subconscious has its marching orders, and often, without a conscious, deliberate effort on your part, you are seizing the small opportunities around you and engaging in the right behaviors that make that mansion outcome possible.

Here are three simple tips for writing an effective self-affirmation:

- Focus on what you do want, not what you don't want. Instead of saying, "My voice doesn't quiver when I talk," you say, "When I speak, my voice is strong and steady."

- Start your affirmation with the words, "I am…" With those simple two words, you have given yourself a name. You must believe it to see it. The "I am…" statement sets the creation in motion. Instead of saying, "I am a nervous speaker," you can substitute it with, "I am a calm, confident speaker, and my voice is strong and steady when I speak."

- Tell the truth in your statement. A lie will be rejected by your subconscious so don't waste your time and effort with one. Almost always, when a person says they tried self-affirmations and they didn't work, it's because they lied to themselves. Instead of saying, "I am a calm, confident speaker, and my voice is strong and steady when I speak," a more effective statement would be, "I am becoming a calm, confident speaker, and my voice is growing stronger and more steady when I speak."

Figure 4: Three Simple Rules

Using your self-affirmation statement

Remember in chapter three I argued that a $5,000 bike wasn't going to win the race for you? That you can't just hop on the bike and magically be an amazing athlete? The right tool is essential to any goal, but you still must use the tool properly and that takes practice. Writing the self-affirmation statement is a start, but if you don't practice using it, then it isn't worth the paper it's written on.

Practice with your self-affirmation statement begins well before you need it. You are counter-balancing your negative thinking and that's no easy task when you consider the percentage of negative thoughts that stream through your brain on any given day. You would be shocked at how high that percentage is. Even for the most positive, optimistic person, it is not a 50/50 split between positive and negative thoughts. We are wired to go to the dark side in our thinking because survival is more likely when we assume danger.

The best way to help you understand this negative bias is to think about a camping trip. You and your friends are sitting around a campfire, enjoying conversation and beverages before going to bed. Suddenly you hear sounds of movement in the forest, just beyond the firelight, and those sounds are getting closer and closer. Without thinking, you are on your feet, looking around for a stick or stone to defend yourself. In your head, you measure the distance to your car. Then, out of the dark and into the light, steps a raccoon that quickly darts back into the dark and scurries away. What did it cost you to assume you were in danger when you were not? Nothing but a few extra calories burned.

Now consider a different response to the sound of movement and its consequences. Instead of being on guard and ready to fight or run, you told yourself and others that the sound was nothing and you continued to enjoy your beverage. But this time a big, black bear stepped out of the dark and into the light. You lost precious seconds of preparation, and those few seconds could mean the difference between life and death.

When we are faced with a change in our environment or an event in which we are not sure of a specific outcome, we are wired to assume that the change or event will harm us. It's a basic survival program we inherited from our ancient ancestors. This program is responsible for the onslaught of negative thinking that constantly streams through our minds. We don't have to be victims of this negativity. We can take control of the stream of thoughts, but it takes a deliberate effort to add positive thoughts to the mix. They won't just happen – it's up to you to create your opportunities.

The best way to create opportunities to counter-balance the negativity is to place your self-affirmation statement in areas where you will see it several times a day. Write the message on a post-it note and place that note beside your computer, next to your coffee machine, and beside your bed. You might take a dry-erase marker and write it on your mirror but be sure it is a dry-erase marker and not a permanent marker! Finally, write the affirmation on the back of a business card and place it in your wallet so that it is easily accessible at any time of the day, no matter where you are. Another really great place to put your self-affirmation statement is on the screensaver of your phone. How often do you look at your phone? If you are like most, it's a lot!

Throughout your day, each time you encounter your statement, don't just look at it, read it. It's most powerful if you say the words out loud so that you are hearing them in addition to reading them. If you are not able to read out loud, then read the words quietly inside your head but pause and think about the words as you are reading them. Ideally, you want to repeat your self-affirmation statement to yourself ten to fifteen times a day. At the very least, read the statement first thing when you get up in the morning and just before you go to bed at night. This sets the tone for the day and it is your last message to your subconscious at the end of the day.

In addition to your daily practice, you will want to read the self-affirmation several times immediately preceding a high-stakes speaking situation. Read it at least three times and pair it with breathing. Your brain can only process one thought at a time. Try talking to a friend on the telephone and answer a question from your child at the same time. It can't be done! You have to switch your focus to think of the right answer or you will find yourself saying yes when you really should have said no. Don't think your child doesn't know this. They all learn this little trick very young.

It's the same thing with the self-affirmation. You can't think positive thoughts simultaneously with negative thoughts. It's one or the other. When you are deliberately focusing on a positive thought and adding golden oxygen to the mix, you are slowing the fight-or-flight responses and literally giving your brain a breather.

Your body is talking to you

What you say to yourself matters but your posture matters, too. It's a chicken and egg situation. How you feel about yourself influences your posture and your posture influences how you feel. It's time to take control. When you are hunched over, taking up as little space as possible, you are communicating to the world and your own subconscious that you are not worthy. Throw your shoulders back and lift your head up. You will feel better about yourself, and others will respond to you with more respect.

Confident people take up space. It is a natural response to success, and it occurs in all cultures. When people achieve something important, they throw their arms up in the air. Interestingly, even people who are blind and therefore have never seen this done, do this too. When you are scared, you hunch your shoulders, stoop a little, and pull your arms in toward your body. It's a universal response. When you are taking up space with legs shoulder-width apart or more, head up and hands on your hips, your brain says, "Hey, we've got this!" And it rewards you with a cocktail of happy hormones.

Amy Cuddy (2018) refers to this stance as the Wonder Woman or Super Man stance, and she recommends that before tackling any challenge, you take three minutes to stand in this position in front of a mirror and repeat your personal self-affirmation. The result will be immediate because your brain recognizes the stance and will respond with a change in the mix of hormones in your body.

If you don't have access to a mirror or others are around, you can approximate the pose. Stand tall or sit up straight. Lift your head. You might focus on a point on the wall to ensure you keep your head up. Keep your arms loosely by your side or resting on the arms of a chair. Subtly, take up as much space as you can. In this position, repeat your self-affirmation in your head for two to three minutes. This will chase away the cortisol in your body and replace it with the DOSE happy chemicals that will help you think more clearly and feel more confident. Add some deep breathing to the mix and you are really helping yourself. Don't simply take my word for it - test it for yourself and discover just how much your posture influences your mood.

Taking back control

When you know what is happening, you can take back control. You might be wired to be on guard and negative thoughts will flow easily, but you can choose to add more positive thoughts into that mix. Adjust your body posture and put your subconscious on notice, emphasizing, "We are worthy, we are confident, and we can do this!" It feels like magic but it's just simple body chemistry used to your advantage.

6

Make It Easier, Recruit Your Whole Brain

"I need some help. I feel like a total mess," Tatum said as she entered my office and plopped down in the recliner.

"What's going on?" I asked.

Tatum responded, "I'm not sleeping, and I feel like I'm not getting much done at work. I can't afford to be unproductive. I've got a big deadline coming, but when I try to work, I just can't focus."

"That's not good, but I've never known you to miss a deadline. What's different right now?"

Slouching deeper into the chair, Tatum explained, "I have to meet with my VP and all the directors next week. I submitted my report on the Baldwin project and they want to go over the details with me."

"That doesn't sound like a bad thing. This is a great opportunity for you to increase your profile with the decision makers. What's the issue? Are you not sure about your numbers?"

"No, I've gone over my numbers and my recommendations a thousand times," Tatum mumbled, with a tone of quiet desperation in her voice. "I know the report is right, I'm just not good at speaking in front of others, especially people higher up. Just thinking about it puts my stomach in knots. I try to distract myself with work or, when I'm home, reading or watching TV, but the picture of myself trying to talk to these people keeps intruding. I just can't stop thinking about it. I feel miserable."

Getting out of your own way

The pioneer psychologist Carl Jung said, "What you resist not only persists, but it will grow in size." Right now, our friend Tatum sees the tension she feels around speaking to authority as something that is wrong and should be escaped. The more she fights this feeling, the more entangled she gets with it. Has this ever happened to you?

Have you ever played with a Chinese Finger Puzzle? You insert your fingers in each end of the puzzle, and the more you pull to remove your fingers, the tighter the cords become. The only way to escape the puzzle is paradoxically to relax. Nongard (2018) describes this experience as being the same as dealing with anything that causes you pain. The only way to escape it is to accept it.

That may not seem right, but do you remember the anxiety-performance curve presented in chapter two? Some anxiety is necessary for optimal performance. Instead of seeing the tension as a bad thing, you can reframe it as your friend. Here is a little exercise, called 'Hot Pen Brainstorming', that can begin that process:

1. Get a notepad, a pen, a high-lighter and a timer.

2. Set your timer for seven minutes.

3. Write for the entire seven minutes, even if you run out of things to write. If it feels like you have run out, just keep writing anything – your grocery list, why you think the exercise is boring, etc. When you get past the low hanging fruit and get past the idea that you have said all that can be said, that is when great material bubbles up. Often, some of your best thoughts will come after you have pushed through the gap.

4. Write your answer to this question:

   "Feeling tense or anxious about speaking in a high-stakes situation is a good thing because…"

   Remember, keep writing for the whole time!

5. After the timer goes off, review your writing. Highlight any key words that seem to be most meaningful to you. Create a short list of three to five words or phrases and write them on a small card, a post-it note, or on your phone's screensaver.

6. Review these words any time you are anticipating a speaking opportunity in which you feel as if you are in the spotlight and you begin to feel your anxiety rising. The goal is not to be rid of the anxiety but rather to put boundaries on it so that it remains in the optimal range.

The trouble with frames

When something happens, we immediately judge it as good/bad, safe/unsafe, or like/dislike and the incident is then stored in our memory with this frame around it. It happens automatically and at lightning speed because it is connected to survival. The sooner we can detect danger, the sooner we can take action to protect ourselves. Your first experience with speaking in front of others was associated with a physical stress response. This was discussed in chapter two. You felt stressed because your emotional brain detected the potential for rejection. If that first experience went well, you associated some positive thoughts to it and put a positive frame around it that balanced the negative stress frame. The next time you had to speak in front of others, the butterflies were a little less intense. With each new successful experience, the positive frame grew bigger and the negative stress frame shrank. Eventually, the stress frame disappeared entirely. Now, you no longer felt those pesky butterflies when you anticipated speaking in front of others. This is the ideal scenario but not the one most people experience.

For most people, the stress response gets bigger, not smaller. For example, Riley is required to give a speech in his seventh-grade language arts class. Riley's response to the assignment is suspicion and caution. He is confronted with a no-win situation. If he doesn't prepare and deliver the speech, he will face rejection and negative consequences from his teacher and parents, who expect him to complete school assignments. If he does write and deliver the speech, his peers (who are also his audience) might judge it negatively. Rejection from his peer group is a dangerous prospect.

Riley chooses to work on writing his speech but does so under a cloud of dread. This emotion of dread gets associated with the already unpleasant experience of the stress response, increasing his level of fear and the negative frame grows. The moment comes when he is standing in front of his peer group.

All systems are on high alert, scanning the environment for any indications of further threat. Tiffany, seated in the third row to Riley's right, sneezes. He jumps nervously but presses on. A sneeze is just a sneeze. Suddenly, Alex shifts in his seat and snorts. Why did he snort? Is that an indication of disgust or does he just need a tissue? Brooke, seated behind Alex, giggles. Riley's mind races, the cortisol surging through his body as part of the stress predisposes him to negative judgments.

Immediately, Riley goes to the dark-side and attaches meaning to Brooke's behavior - she giggled because she thinks I'm stupid or my speech is stupid. The frame gets larger. Distracted by the sequence of the sneeze, snort and giggle, Riley loses his place in his speech. He feels the panic rising. Now everyone will see that he isn't good at this speech-giving thing. The frame gets even bigger.

This negative sequence would be bad enough if it were restricted to just speech-making, but we humans have an important skill called 'generalizing.'   If the growing negative frame for speech-making was just about speech-making, then Riley could simply avoid making speeches for his entire life and everything would be fine. Unfortunately, that isn't what happens.

As a species, we are very good at detecting patterns and associating them with previous patterns. That allows us to detect threats in situations that are not exactly like a previous threat and to take proactive action. When we do that, we are more likely to survive, so that is a good thing - most of the time. In many cases, something happens, and we scan our many frames that we have stored over the years and hang the new incident on an old frame. This usually works just fine.

However, when that frame was built on a misjudgment, as it probably was in Riley's response to Brooke's giggle, that can be counter-productive. The old frame grew based on an exaggerated judgment of a threat, and now that frame is changing how we see the new event. Anything that is similar to speech-making can be attached to this frame. Now, giving a toast at a wedding, providing a eulogy for a loved one, presenting an idea to your team, or being interviewed for a job are all being responded to with the original speech-making frame. If you look for rejection, you will find it and being hyper-vigilant to this will cause you to find evidence that you are being judged as 'not good enough.' The frame continues to grow.

Our natural response to this downward spiral of despair is to avoid any situation that is reminiscent of the original speech-making frame. Unfortunately, that doesn't work because each time you are confronted with the potential of having to speak in front of others, the faulty frame is pulled up from your memory bank. In your mind, you are applying the frame to the potential situation. Just thinking about it, makes your heart race. That pesky frame has set off your stress response because your mind doesn't differentiate between an actual event and a vivid picture of the event. That's why you tear up watching a sad movie and why you don't have to experience a high-stakes speaking event to feel the fear. Each time you experience the fear response, whether the experience is real or just imagined, the frame grows.

Your details will be different from Riley's, but the process is the same. If your first response to a high-stakes speaking situation is to look for the door, then you were probably exposed to some highly emotional, negative experiences that have put you on this downward spiral of fear. Reversing the spiral so that speaking in the spotlight is less uncomfortable will require a deliberate interruption of the program running in your head.

Dehypnotizing yourself

Hypnosis is an inside job. You do it to yourself. Hollywood has created many misconceptions about hypnosis that need to be clarified. Hypnosis is simply focused attention that is accompanied by reduced peripheral awareness and an enhanced capacity to respond to suggestions. When you are hypnotized, you are in a trance-state of mind in which your executive function, your conscious brain, is no longer controlling your thoughts or actions.

All hypnosis is self-hypnosis and you go in and out of trances all day long. When you are reading a story, you put yourself into the story, and you are imagining the context in which the hero is interacting. If you are deep into the story, you might lose track of time. I have burned the potatoes while reading many, many times. While watching an exciting football or baseball game, you might lose awareness of your immediate surroundings and find your heart pounding as you wait for the outcome of the next pitch or the next play. You can be lost in thought as you drive home after a busy day at work. As you pull into your driveway you might notice that you have no recall of certain turns or passing particular buildings along your route. Yet, you must have, because here you are, at home. Trances are a natural state and they are happening all the time.

While most trances are harmless and some are even helpful in that they give your conscious, judging brain a break, Riley's downward spiral is not harmless. When he slips into this trance, it is getting in the way of his ability to speak in a high-stakes situation. His stress response is activated by just thinking about speaking in a high-stakes condition. Given the actual threat present in his environment, his fear response is at an exaggerated level, but like a very dark pair of sunglasses, it's coloring everything Riley is experiencing. To escape this distorted view and to return to clear, productive thinking, Riley must de-hypnotize himself.

If Riley's story is like yours, and I am willing to bet it is, then you too will need to dehypnotize yourself. How do you do that? It's so much easier than you might expect. If you have hypnotized yourself into responding to high-stakes speaking situations with fear, you can also hypnotize yourself into responding with calm and confidence.

Deliberate self-hypnosis

I said earlier that hypnosis involves focused attention that is produced by reducing your peripheral awareness. The result is that your conscious mind, that part of your mind that is logical and rational, goes offline and your subconscious mind takes over. Any thoughts you have in this state are bypassing your critical faculty, the conscious mind, and are accessing the subconscious mind directly. This explains why, under hypnosis, your capacity to respond to suggestions is enhanced. According to the suggestion, these thoughts become the marching orders for your subconscious mind, and they influence your perceptions and behaviors.

Without being aware of it, you are hypnotizing yourself all the time. You can take control of this haphazard occurrence by using any one of several tools to deliberately re-program your subconscious. Any strategy you use that puts you in a relaxed state of full absorption will open the door to your subconscious and enhance your suggestibility. You can listen to soothing music, enjoy the sound and smells of ocean waves as they roll in, watch a cloud drift by, or listen to the birds chirping in your backyard feeder. The possibilities are endless.

To deliberately re-program your mind, breathe deeply and focus on a pleasant, non-demanding, leisurely stimuli. Close your eyes if you are in a safe place to do so. While you are focused on your breathing and whatever you have chosen to watch or imagine, your mind will wander because that is what minds do. As a thought enters your mind, you can notice you are having a thought and then let it go and re-focus your attention on your breath and whatever else you have chosen. After a couple of minutes, you will feel more relaxed. When that happens, you can focus on a positive thought. If you have prepared a self-affirmation statement, repeat that to yourself now. When your subconscious is more open to suggestions, as it is now, that self-affirmation statement has additional power to influence your behavior. Enjoy this internal video of you being successful, calm, and confident in your high-stakes speaking situation. When you are ready you can smile and return to your day feeling more composed and prepared for your event.

There are many free or inexpensive tools available on the internet or your smart phone's app store that can guide you into this state of relaxed openness to suggestion. You can search for terms such as mindfulness, meditation, progressive relaxation or self-hypnosis. All these tools operate in a similar manner, so it is worth experimenting until you find something that works for you. As my gift to you, go to www.ICanspeakbook.com. You can download a recording and enjoy a self-hypnosis session that is specifically focused on maintaining calmness and confidence in any situation in which all eyes are on you. There is an advantage to having a recording such as this on your smart phone. Since your phone is usually within easy reach, you can access the recording anywhere and whenever you need it most. The more often you listen to a self-hypnosis recording such as this one, the stronger its influence becomes.

While self-hypnosis feels like magic, it really isn't. Your limbic system, which is referred to as the emotional brain, is just more powerful than your conscious brain. We like to think we make most of our decisions with our conscious, logical, rational brain, but that just isn't true. Your subconscious mind is constantly at work, scanning your environment for opportunities to execute whatever programs you have installed and changing your perceptions according to those programs. Why not take back control by uninstalling those programs that are getting in your way and re-programing your brain with more helpful suggestions? By deliberately using self-hypnosis, you can now recruit your emotional brain, your subconscious, to help your conscious brain achieve your goals. You are now firing on all cylinders!

7
Seeing It

"I just can't see it," Cam said. "I just can't do it."

"What can't you do?" I asked.

He replied with frustration, "My boss wants me to present the rationale for our new project to the entire software committee. I just can't see myself doing it!"

"Do you agree with what you are being asked to present?"

With much more energy, Cam said, "Absolutely! This is an important project, and people need to understand its value. If we implement the project, it could launch us into a very profitable market."

I responded, "But you can't see yourself presenting to the software committee, right? What *do* you see when you think of presenting?"

"I see a lot of frowns and shaking heads, people dozing off or looking at their phones," he answered.

I shifted my legs and leaned forward in my chair. "Oh, so you *do* see yourself making the presentation. It just isn't a very pretty picture, right?"

Cam squirmed, "Yeah, I do see it. I just don't want to put myself in that picture."

Your mind and pictures

Cam's resistance to putting himself in what he predicts will be an unpleasant and probably unsuccessful situation makes a lot of sense. Energy is a scarce resource. Why invest energy into something that is not going to produce a positive outcome? The problem for Cam is not that he is being asked to make a presentation. The problem is the negative picture he has in his head.

The mind doesn't separate events that have happened from vivid pictures of an event. Have you ever had a bad dream where someone you know has done something to hurt you? When you wake up, even though you know that the event was a dream and not real, how do you feel when you encounter that person later in the day? Are you angry with that person? Do you have to consciously remind yourself that the person has not actually harmed you?

Recently, I bought a puppy. I have a vivid picture of standing beside the breeder's desk while he reviewed the puppy's history of shots and explained what food the puppy was used to eating. I remember seeing a pen that was behind the breeder that had several bouncing, active, happy puppies and the door that let out to his kitchen. I even remember him handing me a starter kit of food and potty pads. The interesting thing about this memory is that it didn't happen. My friend picked the puppy up for me. I was never there. My friend used FaceTime so I could talk to the breeder. I don't remember watching all of this via my smart phone, rather, I remember *being there*!

A vivid picture in your mind gets stored the same way an actual event gets stored. Any good lawyer knows that. They ask a dozen seemingly insignificant questions, many of them leading questions, to get you to create that vivid picture. With the right questions they can install the right memory and blur or confuse your actual memory of the real event. In that way, the attorney can create the testimony that will be most helpful to their case. It is well known in the legal world that an eyewitness isn't very reliable.

Self-hypnosis and guided visualization

In the previous chapter, I made a case for self-hypnosis. Guided visualization is a special subset of self-hypnosis that can be particularly useful for high-stakes speaking. You can re-program your mind with words. But an even faster way to re-program your brain is to use a picture. The second habit listed in Stephen Covey's popular book, *The Seven Habits of Highly Effective People*, is to begin with the end in mind. Guided visualization helps you to do that by guiding you to a picture of your success.

There are two ways to enjoy guided visualization. You can search the internet or download an app with generic recordings of guided visualizations. These generic experiences will interrupt the negative thoughts and guide your mind to focus on imagining uplifting scenes. In doing so, your brain increases the production of all the happy hormones, particularly serotonin. The result is the chemistry in your brain has changed to have less cortisol and more of the neurotransmitters that are more pleasant and conducive to clear thinking. It's like giving your mind a little vacation. Go to www.ICanspeakbook.com, and you can experience a generic guided visualization. I have provided two versions. Enjoy them both!

The other way to use guided visualization is to create a very clear picture of what success looks like for you and how you can achieve that success. The best way is to begin with a pen, paper and a timer. Use the hot pen method of brainstorming described in chapter two. Set the time for seven minutes and begin writing. Use the who, what, when, where, and how approach to detailing the situation as it is unfolds and after it has ended.

The more specific you can be, the better. You might even describe what you are wearing, what smells are in the air, what sounds are in the background, and what the temperature of the room is. Imagine who is with you and whether they are standing or sitting. How far are they from you? Describe their smiles and their nods of approval. Be sure to describe the applause or congratulations you will receive after the event is completed. Will it be in person, or will you receive notes or emails? As a result of what you said, what are other people now saying?

Be sure to write for the whole seven minutes and don't worry if you jump forward and then go backward in time. Spelling and grammar don't count in this exercise so just keep writing. When you are done, review what you have written and highlight the most important points.

Now comes the fun part. Take your rough brainstorming notes and write a cohesive description of the future event. Your description will have a clear sequence, beginning with the start of the event and finishing with a clear picture of the positive results you will experience. Since the only one who is going to see this is you, spelling and grammar still don't count, so enjoy the writing process!

Once you have completed your description and you are satisfied that it is thorough, you can go to www.ICanspeakbook.com. I have provided a simple self-hypnosis induction that will help you get into the relaxed state that is most advantageous to self-hypnosis. Part way through the recording, you will be instructed to hit the pause button, open your eyes, and read your personal guided image of success. If you are in a place where you can read this out loud, that will add to the exercise's effectiveness, but it is not essential. Once you have read your personal guided image, you can turn the recording back on and finish your experience. If you are comfortable with recording equipment, you might consider creating your own audio recording of your script.

Repetition is the key. The more often you visualize your success, the calmer and more confident you will be when it comes time to execute the high-stakes conversation or presentation. It doesn't matter whether you use a generic guided visualization or you build your personal guided visualization, tailored to the exact situation you are anticipating. Either experience will leave you feeling more positive, energized, and less stressed - which is certainly a good thing!

8
Changing Beliefs

"That was a great session. I took a bunch of notes, and there are several ideas I can use as soon as I get back to the office," Sam said excitedly.

Wade responded, "I felt the same way. This has been a great conference. Thanks for suggesting I register."

"Are you going to the social tonight?" Sam asked. "They always have great snacks, and they're giving away a lot of really cool stuff. Just the Amazon gift card alone is worth showing up for!"

Wade looked away and then returned his attention to Sam. "I don't know about that. I'm kind of tired and besides, I never know what to say at these things."

Getting to the source

There could be any number of reasons for Wade's hesitance to attend a networking event at a conference. Chances are, however, at least one, and perhaps several, irrational beliefs are at the source of all the other reasons. Most conferences have a mixer or social event, and they do so because they create opportunities for serendipitous connections. The purpose is to allow conference attendees an opportunity to share learning, develop additional resources, and build relationships. Given the potential for so many benefits, it would be logical for folks to love these events, right? Well sadly, there are many people who, like Wade, find excuses to avoid them.

Irrational beliefs don't just affect our willingness to attend conference mixers. They are also responsible for most of the anxiety you feel about any of the other high-stakes speaking contexts. In chapter four, I explained self-talk and how important it is to maintain positive thoughts. Irrational beliefs are feeding your negativity, so it is time to get past the symptoms and address the source.

Irrational beliefs

Albert Ellis, the father of Rational Emotive Behavior Therapy (REBT), believed that irrational beliefs were the reason for human misery and dysfunction. Irrational beliefs are beliefs that are unhelpful, illogical, and inconsistent with our social reality. They are those ideas you have about yourself that don't match your reality. They can be ideas about yourself, about others or about the world in general. They produce "I-you-they should…," or "I-you-they have to…" thoughts and they impose expectations and conditions that are impossible to meet. Irrational beliefs trick you into feeling bad about yourself, others, or the world in general because they distort reality. It's like walking around in your own dark cloud that colors all that you see in a dull grey.

Ellis' A-B-C of irrational beliefs

The stoic philosopher, Epictetus, said, "It's not what happens to you, but how you react to it that matters" (Stanhope, 2016). That philosophy is at the base of Ellis' approach to counseling. In his years of practice, he observed some consistent patterns of belief that were not connected to reality and were causing his patients' emotional pain. According to Ellis (1975), "you mainly feel the way you think." Given that, if you change your thinking, you will change how you feel.

Irrational beliefs, according to Ellis, are developed in an A-B-C sequence. Something happens that is either unpleasant or a challenge, which he labeled as an **A**dversity. You attach meaning to the event, and that meaning can be either positive or negative, which then determines the **B**elief you have about that adversity. If the meaning you attached to the adversity was negative, then the **C**onsequence will be self-defeating or dysfunctional behavior. If instead, you attach a positive meaning and you now have a healthy belief about the adversity, then the consequence will be functional and will promote a sense of optimism.

Figure 5: ABC's of Belief

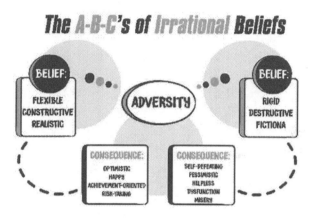

It's easy to see how this sequence might play out for a high-stakes speaking situation. A normal response to any situation in which you feel your performance will be judged is to feel some level of anxiety and, as discussed in chapter two, some level of anxiety is a good thing. However, if your attached meaning to your physical responses to the challenge is that you shouldn't feel this way, then the consequence is likely to be the avoidance of similar situations in the future. Instead, you might recognize that the physical sensations you are experiencing are helping you stay focused and you can put in the right effort to enable your best performance.

With this belief, you will tackle the challenge with energy and confidence. Your outcome has a high probability of being more successful than with a negative belief, and you will approach future high-stakes situations with optimism.

To put yourself in this more functional, happier mindset you need to become consciously aware of the subconscious beliefs that are fueling your thoughts. Ellis identified the twelve most common irrational beliefs:

1. I need love and approval from those significant to me.

2. To feel happy and be worthwhile, I must achieve and succeed at whatever I do and make no mistakes.

3. People should always do the right thing. When they behave obnoxiously, unfairly, or selfishly, they must be blamed and punished.

4. Things must be the way I want them to be; otherwise, life will be intolerable.

5. My unhappiness is caused by things that are outside my control, so there is little I can do to feel any better.

6. I must worry about things that could be dangerous, unpleasant, or frightening; otherwise, they might happen.

7. I can be happier by avoiding life's difficulties, unpleasantness, and responsibilities.

8. Everyone needs to depend on someone stronger than themselves.

9. Events in my past are the cause of my problems, and they continue to influence my feelings and behaviors now.

10. I should become upset when other people have problems and feel unhappy when they are sad.

11. I shouldn't have to feel discomfort and pain. I can't stand discomfort and pain, and I must avoid them at all costs.

12. Every problem should have an ideal solution, and it is intolerable when one can't be found.

After reviewing the list of twelve irrational beliefs, it is likely that at least one of them resonates with you. Almost everyone has accepted at least one of these beliefs and it is quite probable that you have accepted more than one. It is the degree to which these beliefs are influencing your thoughts and behavior that is the issue.

For example, I know that I am influenced by number two on this list: *"To feel happy and be worthwhile, I must achieve and succeed at whatever I do and make no mistakes."* That's what keeps me pushing to get better and better at things that I value. It's what gets me up at five in the morning to tap on my keyboard until it's time to get ready for my day's work. It's also what influences me to research my ideas and to have my work professionally edited and proofread. To that extent, the belief is functional. However, if I get too entrenched in the belief, I won't risk starting projects for fear of failure. In my work with businesspeople at all levels of their organization, I have encountered many gifted thinkers that have put off important projects for fear that they might not succeed or that others will be critical of their effort.

It isn't hard to recognize yourself in any of these beliefs, but if you would like to take an assessment to confirm your suspicions or to understand to what degree you are committed to them, you can go to: http://www.testandcalc.com/Self_Defeating_Beliefs/questtxt.asp. This assessment provides an informal look, but it is interesting. If you score a six or higher on any of these items, you might want to apply the following instructions to help you replace your irrational beliefs with more functional, helpful ones.

Using the A-B-C-D-E to change beliefs

While awareness is an essential first and big step toward taking back control and living your best self, sadly it is not enough. It is a necessary but not sufficient on its own. In fact, if you stop here and do nothing more, completing the A-B-C and arriving at a new awareness could easily become counter-productive because it will be just one more reason to be critical of yourself. In chapter four I discussed the influence of what you say to yourself has on your outcomes. You cannot afford to stop at simple awareness. You need to take the next steps. Albert Ellis firmly believed that if you take these steps, you can change those beliefs.

To change your beliefs, according to Ellis' model, you must **D**ispute them. This means that you challenge the belief by asking, is this a rational thought? What evidence is there that supports this belief as the truth?

Confirmation bias works to support our irrational beliefs by filtering out any evidence that is contradictory and highlighting any experience that supports the belief. To dispute the irrational belief, you must deliberately look for contradictory evidence that you have not noticed in the past. Returning to challenge my problematic belief, *"To feel happy and be worthwhile, I must achieve and succeed at whatever I do and make no mistakes,"* I could ask myself the following questions:

- Why must I achieve and succeed at whatever I do and make no mistakes?

- Have I ever made a mistake and still felt like I was a worthwhile person?

- Have I ever known anyone who never made a mistake? Is it possible to live a life without ever making a mistake?

- When others make a mistake, do I write them off as not being worthwhile people?

- Why am I kinder to others than to myself?

- Why should I expect to be the one exception in the world that never makes a mistake?

- What is the cost of accepting this belief? What am I missing out on?

- What risks am I not taking because I am afraid that I might not succeed? Is staying safe worth the cost?

The number of dispute questions I can ask myself can go on and on, but you get the idea. This line of questions helps you to recognize the irrationality of the belief consciously. It would be funny except the belief has had some very real and negative consequences for you. When you can see the irrationality, it can leave you feeling sad that you have allowed this unfounded belief to waste your energy and act as a barrier to accomplishing things that really matter to you.

After disputing the irrational belief, it's time to replace it with a more **E**ffective new philosophy. There are different ways you can do this, but I recommend sitting down and writing a letter to yourself. Set a timer and write for at least five minutes. Here is a summarized letter I might write to myself:

Dear Paula,

Living a life with no mistakes isn't possible and trying to do so is costing you dearly. It's time to change that. You can try things and, if you make a mistake, you can correct it. That's how you learn and get better. Trying to avoid making mistakes is getting in the way of your doing some important things. If you are honest with yourself, you succeed much more often than you fail. You need to give yourself more credit for your successes. Take time to notice them or the only thing you will think about are the few mistakes you have made along the way. You need to put them in the right perspective, so they don't drain your energy and make you afraid of taking risks. Letting go of the need to succeed will free you up to enjoy the journey, so just let it go.

Love,

Paula

I realize that this might seem a little silly, especially if you have never done anything like it before. Try it and you'll see how you feel when you are done. I promise you, writing it will be freeing. Once written, you should read it back to yourself at least once a day for a week. As you read it to yourself, feel free to add to it or change it. Make it a living document, but it *must* be a kind document. Take the same care and gentleness you might use if you were writing to a child and lace it with hope and encouragement.

Once you have your letter to yourself and have used it for a week, you are now ready to summarize it into a succinct self-affirmation statement. Use the guides for writing a good affirmation statement that were shared in chapter four. Once again, you will need to practice the statement. To do that, put it in places where you will see it. In chapter four, I gave you several ideas of places you could post your self-affirmation statement. My favorite is using a dry-erase marker to write it on my mirror. When I write it on my mirror, it is one of the first things I see in the morning. What a great way to start my day!

Thought-stopping

There is another way to install more effective beliefs, and that is to use a thought-stopping tool. When you are anticipating a high-stakes speaking event and you begin to feel that familiar anxiety rising, notice the thoughts running through your head.

Since you now know which of the twelve irrational beliefs are haunting you, you can ask yourself, which belief is at the source of this anxiety right now. Next, visualize a stop sign and yell "STOP" to yourself. If you are in a place where you can do this out loud, do so. If not, just yell it to yourself inside your mind.

Then, deliberately replace the unhealthy thought with the opposite thought. Breathe slowly and deeply while you repeat your more healthy, opposite thought. For example, if you catch yourself saying to yourself, "This is going to be awful. I'm going to embarrass myself," replace it with the thought, "This is going to be fine. I

will say and do things that will reflect *well* on me."
Whatever your thought, change it to exactly the opposite
and repeat it to yourself several times. If the negative
thought creeps back in, return to your opposite thought
and say it, either out loud or internally, with more energy,
faster and louder.

Thought-stopping works because you can only think
about one thing at a time. We all like to believe that we
are multi-taskers, but that is impossible. We are multi-
switchers not multi-taskers. Our brain switches from
one task to the next, sometimes at a very fast pace. When
we switch, some data gets lost and the more frequently
we switch from the unhealthy thought to the more
optimistic thought, the weaker the unhealthy thought
becomes.

When we use thought-stopping, we are literally re-wiring
our brains because if we are thinking a positive thought,
we cannot possibly be thinking a weak thought. The
more frequently our brain processes the stronger
thought, the stronger the path in our brain becomes.
You have heard the phrase, "use it or lose it." The brain
trims the paths that are not being used. That's why you
can't remember how to solve complex math equations
or your high school Spanish! Unless you have a reason
to regularly use these skills, your brain trimmed the paths
to make room for newer, more frequently used
information. Since thought-stopping prevents you from
traveling the dysfunctional unhealthy path, it gets
trimmed over time.

Thought-stopping also works to calm you in the moment because it disrupts the pattern. The previous sequence of thinking the thought and then your body going on high alert cannot occur because you are immediately replacing the unhealthy thought with a calming thought. By stopping the dysfunctional thought, you can slow down or completely shut down the fight-or-flight response. The slow, deep breathing adds to the positive message because it is the opposite breathing pattern to the one used when you are in fight-or-flight mode. The brain now has additional oxygen with which to process thoughts and a dual message, your deliberate positive thought and the calm breathing, that indicates all is well.

Words are powerful

Words matter and, depending on the words you use, they will change your future. What we say to ourselves is what we do. If you are telling yourself there is reason to be anxious, you are going to be anxious. If you tell yourself you are going to succeed, your subconscious will help you to say and do the things necessary for that success. Now that you understand which irrational beliefs are at the base of the script your subconscious is currently using, you can deliberately replace that script with either a tailored self-affirmation statement or thought-stopping. Ideally, you will combine them. You can use the thought-stopping tool and then follow it with a self-affirmation statement. There is no need to continue to suffer with a dysfunctional, irrational script. The choice is yours.

9
Move Your Body!

"Stop it!" Anna demanded.

"Stop what?" Carrie asked.

"Do you really not know? Your knee, it's bouncing and it's making me nervous."

Carrie explained, "I can't help it, it's what happens when I get nervous. I love Riley and I want to give the toast, but I am just so nervous." She placed her hand on her knee to still the movement.

"You have your speech, right? And everyone here knows and loves you. So, what's the issue?" Anna asked.

"Yeah, the speech is right here," Carrie responded as she tapped the purse she had set on the table. "I just get worried that the words won't come out right. I think it makes it worse that everyone knows me."

"You're doing it again," Anna said with exasperation.

Managing the adrenaline

Has this ever happened to you? You're feeling anxious about a spotlight speaking situation and you discover your knee is bouncing, your hand is tapping, or you are fidgeting with some object in your hand. If you are standing, perhaps you can't help pacing? All these physical movements are a normal response to the adrenaline flooding your body. The fight-or-flight response prepares you to run away or face the threat head-on and fight it. Since you are not doing either, all that nervous energy needs to escape. The bouncing, tapping, fidgeting, and pacing are the result.

These behaviors, however, are a problem. When you give in to them, they don't calm you down; instead, they serve to maintain the heightened alert. Their presence is a continuous reminder to your brain that a threat is present and heightened vigilance is necessary. If you want to perform at your best in a high-stakes situation, it is necessary to slow or eliminate these behaviors. Fortunately, there are four strategies available to you. They are all effective so you can choose any one of them that feels comfortable to you or better yet, you can combine them to increase control. The four strategies are:

- Gross motor movement;

- Stretching;

- Power pose; and,

- Progressive relaxation.

Gross motor movement

You might ask, isn't gross motor movement the same as pacing? The answer is, yes, on the surface they are the same thing. The difference is you are consciously in control of the movements and they are done with purpose.

Instead of pacing, you can take a walk. If possible, take a short walk outside. Focusing for five minutes, breathing in fresh air will be enough to calm your spirits. Pay attention to your surroundings and truly see everything around you. Being mindful for five minutes will help you to put your challenge in a better perspective. If you can't go outside, walk indoors with a mindful focus. Another option is to climb the same set of stairs four or five times. If you can't walk around and there are no stairs handy, stand up and lift your knees as high as you can for five minutes. You can also engage your upper body in gross motor movement. Spread your arms out like an airplane and make large circles with them or raise them up or down.

It doesn't really matter which gross motor behavior you choose to engage in, because they all do the same thing. They allow the nervous energy to be released while getting more oxygen into your system. Being mindful of the behaviors you are deliberately engaging in shifts your focus away from the event you are anxious about. With this change in focus and additional oxygen, your mind can calm and you can begin thinking more clearly. Go ahead and be creative about your gross motor movement. If anyone asks what you are doing, you can explain you are doing a moving meditation!

Stretching

When you get anxious, your muscles tighten up. Stretching helps to loosen and release the tension in your muscles. It improves circulation throughout your body, feeding all your cells with needed oxygen. When you stretch, your heart rate slows, and your blood pressure decreases. Your brain waves follow your heart rate so they too, slow down to a more relaxed rate. All these benefits make stretching a very good choice. There are many stretches you can use to help you deal with your anxiety. The following are a few of my favorites. Each stretch should be held for 20-30 seconds and repeated two to four times.

Crescent stretch:

Sit with your back straight and reach your arms above your head. Interlock your hands. As you take a deep breath, stretch your arms to the right. Exhale and return your arms to the straight-up position. Inhale and stretch your arms to the left. Exhale and return to the neutral position.

Neck roll:

Sit with your back straight. As you Inhale, stretch your right ear to your right shoulder, keeping the shoulder in a lowered position. Exhale and roll your head toward the center of your chest. Inhale again. As you inhale, stretch your left ear to your left shoulder. Exhale and roll your head toward the center of your chest.

Seated spinal twist

Choose a chair that does not have arms. Sit with your back straight and your feet flat on the floor. Position yourself so that you are sitting toward the edge of the seat. Sit toward the edge of your chair with your feet flat on the floor. Place your right hand at the back of the chair and your left hand on your right thigh. Then inhale, and as you inhale, straighten your back. Exhale and rotate your torso to the right, looking over your right shoulder. Hold this position for 20-30 seconds. Now do the same, in reverse, on your left side.

Chest opener

Stretch your arms out behind your back and clasp your hands. Inhale and squeeze your shoulder blades toward each other and push out your chest. Exhale and release your shoulder blades.

Power pose

The third strategy for managing nervous energy is one that was discussed in chapter four. Any position that allows you to take up more space is going to deliver a strong message to yourself and to others that you are in control. It may not always be possible to slip away to a private spot to engage in a Superwoman/Superman pose but you can always focus on standing up straight, lifting your chin, and throwing your shoulders back. Another small adaptation to the power pose is to stand behind two chairs and place one hand on each of the two chairs. This forces your arms and legs away from your main body and helps you to take up more space. All these poses help ensure good posture, and they also allow you to expand your chest and take in more precious oxygen.

Amy Cuddy also found in her studies that holding a power pose for just two minutes will increase your testosterone by 20%. This alone will help you to feel more aggressive and in control but, in addition, her studies demonstrated that it also decreased cortisol in the bloodstream by 20%. A lower amount of cortisol translates to feeling calmer! Not a bad result for a two-minute investment in time. Add a positive "I am…" statement to that and you are multiplying the positive effect.

Progressive relaxation

Of the four strategies you can use to calm your nervous energy, this one is my favorite because it produces the deepest level of relaxation. It involves tensing and tightening one muscle group at a time and then relaxing the muscles. The alternation of tensing and relaxing helps you to recognize what relaxation of the muscle group feels like and it emphasizes the sense of relaxation. The result is lower blood pressure, a slower heart rate, and your brain waves slowing to the calmer end of the beta range.

Steps to progressive relaxation:

1. Begin by finding a quiet place where you will not be disturbed. Most people enjoy this more if they are lying down but a comfortable chair will do.

2. Begin with your deep, beach ball breathing, and close your eyes.

3. Focus on your forehead, squeezing the muscles for 15 seconds. You can feel the muscles getting tighter and tenser as you continue to focus on them. Slowly release the muscles while counting to 30. Notice the difference as your forehead becomes completely relaxed.

4. Repeat step three for all the other muscle groups in the following sequence: jaw and cheeks, neck and shoulders, arms and hands, buttocks, legs, and feet. It's ok if you miss one muscle group or do them out of order. Generally, it is most comfortable if you start at the top of your head and move downwards with a logical flow.

5. When all muscle groups have been tensed and released, take a minute or two to just enjoy the feeling of relaxation across your entire body. Continue to breathe deeply and slowly. When you are ready to continue your activities, open your eyes, and feel the sense of calm that is now present.

It's not difficult to implement a progressive relaxation session on your own, but if you would prefer, there are many options for a guided experience. You can go to YouTube or search for an app. There are many available at low to no cost. You can also go to www.ICanspeakbook.com and download a recording I have made for you. This recording will guide you through the entire process, and it includes soothing music with the instructions. If you download it to your smart phone, you will have it easily accessible whenever you need it.

There are times when either the environment is not right or you just don't have the time, for a full progressive relaxation experience. When you are in a situation like this, you can use the abbreviated version below. I like to use this when I need a mental break from work. It takes only a few minutes and I can do it at my desk. Although it is very brief, it never fails to leave me feeling refreshed and calm.

Steps to brief progressive relaxation

1. Make yourself as comfortable as possible. If you are seated, place your feet firmly on the ground, about waist distance apart. Rest your arms on your lap or on the arms of your chair. Support your head on the chair's headrest if there is one. If not, let your head fall forward slightly.

2. Begin breathing slowly and deeply.

3. As you inhale, tighten the muscles around your eyes and your cheeks. Hold this position for 15 seconds, increasing the tension as much as you can while you are counting. When you reach 15, exhale and relax all the muscles in your face. Notice the difference. Repeat twice more.

4. Turn your attention to your hands and arms. Inhale and tighten your fist. As you do this, increase the tension in your entire arm. Count to 15, increasing the tension as you count. Exhale and relax your hands and arms. Repeat twice more.

5. Finish with three more deep breaths and enjoy!

Enjoy the calm

Any of the four strategies for releasing nervous energy will leave you feeling physically calmer. They are all free, and none of them have any adverse side-effects! Experiment with them to see which of the four strategies works best for you.

If by chance, your doctor has prescribed an anti-anxiety medication for you, you can still use any of these tools. They will not interfere with your prescription, but they might increase its effectiveness. Many doctors strongly encourage their patients to use these techniques daily, along with their medication. So, whether you are taking medication or not, you have nothing to lose and, potentially, very much to gain.

10
Get Some Help

"What's the matter?" Lance asked as he entered the company café. Daryl was sitting at the table, writing furiously on a pad of paper, his face scrunched up in a frown. His lunch was in front of him on the table, untouched and getting cold.

Daryl looked dejected. "I've got to get this right," he said. "Rebecca is out sick today and I have to deliver her training module to the new employees this afternoon. I'm not Rebecca. The trainees always love her because she is so funny, but I can't pull that off. They are going to hate me."

Lance responded with a smile, "What do you mean, hate you? You know this stuff better than Rebecca. You'll be fine."

"It's not about what I know. It's about my delivery. I'm going to talk and they're going to stare at me with blank faces, or worse, they'll be on their phones texting to each other about how bored they are," Daryl answered.

"So, what are you doing now?" asked Lance.

"I'm trying to rework some of Rebecca's notes so that they will sound more like me but better. Only it's not working. This is going to be bad," Daryl said with some desperation.

Lance replied, "I don't think it's going to be as bad as you expect. But here, let me have a look. Maybe I can help you."

They are not the enemy

Clearly, Daryl lacks self-confidence in his facilitation skills as a trainer. Unfortunately, this lack of confidence will show up in his delivery, and his workshop participants will react to it. The self-fulfilling prophecy is going to come into play here. Participants are going to behave exactly the way Lance expects them to behave and the result will be that his confidence will dip even lower. That downward spiral to despair is in action!

While Daryl's lack of self-confidence is certainly an issue, it isn't the real problem. The real problem is how Daryl is viewing his audience. He is seeing them as the 'enemy.' From his perspective, his audience is hostile and threatening and that feeds his fears which then erodes any confidence he may have had. Does that sound like you? When you are in a high-stakes speaking situation, do you see others who might be evaluating your words as negatively biased against you?

Have you ever attended a conference presentation hoping that the speaker was boring and that you would get nothing out of the session? Unless you are a masochist, of course not. You and the speaker share a mutual purpose. The speaker wants to give you some information and share some ideas with you, and you are there because you want to learn and to get some new ideas. It's the same situation when you are at a wedding. You want the person giving a toast to be successful. When I interview someone for a job, I want to hire the right person. Given that, if you have the right qualifications, I really want you to show me that you have what I need. I want you to be comfortable enough to put your best foot forward. It doesn't matter what the high-stakes situation is. The other people, the ones you believe are judging your performance, are biased in your favor, *not* against you. It is in their best interests that you are comfortable and able to perform at your best. They are not your enemy; you are your own worst enemy. It is your attitude toward them that is causing you stress. Let it go and reframe your audience as your friend and ally.

Recognize that they want you to do well. Breathe deeply and let the best version of yourself shine.

Get over yourself

You can change your focus from you to others. Your brain can only process one thought at a time. Test it for yourself. You cannot add 314 + 93 while also recalling your birthday. It's impossible. You have to do one and then the other. You might recall your birthday with lightning speed, but you had to wait to sequence the tasks. You cannot do them at the same time. This can help you with your anxiety. If you are focused on meeting your audience's need, of providing them with information that will be helpful, then you cannot be focused on your own needs.

The more you focus on others, the less you will focus on yourself. If you are not thinking about yourself and how you are being perceived, you are no longer stoking the fire of insecurity and your stress response can ease up. Make your networking event all about helping others to feel more comfortable. Focus on providing useful information in your presentation to more senior decision-makers or when giving a speech. Make honoring the subject of your toast or eulogy your priority. Try to understand what challenges your interviewer is facing and how the successful applicant can make the interviewer's job easier. No matter what the high-stakes speaking situation, you can take the other person's perspective to understand how you can be helpful to them.

Get help from your friends

A few years ago, I was interviewing candidates for a position in my department. There were four well-qualified candidates. A fifth candidate, Kim, had served as an intern in our department a couple of years earlier and, out of courtesy, I added her to the interview list. She didn't have the experience or the education that the other candidates had so she was a long shot, at best. The day before the interview she recruited her mom to help her prepare. Her mom asked her question after question and gave Kim feedback on her answers. When Kim arrived for the interview, she knew she was ready. She was focused, determined, and calm. There was no question in the minds of the interview team members that she was the best prepared candidate and, based on that interview, I absolutely believed she could do the job and would do it with passion. It was hard to explain to our recruiting department why I selected her over the more experienced candidates, but she has demonstrated every day since, that I made a very smart decision.

With any high-stakes speaking situation, your friends and family can be a great emotional support. They can also be a great help in providing helpful feedback and additional guidance. Ken Blanchard once said, "Feedback is the breakfast of champions." Your friends and family are on your side and looking out for you.

Their feedback will be given with the best of intentions because they want you to succeed. Think of their feedback as your safety net. With it, you can clean up your content and practice your delivery, knowing that it is getting better and better.

Join a group

There is nothing like experience to improve a skill and to build confidence. The more you practice speaking with all eyes on you, the more comfortable it will become. It doesn't matter which of the spotlight speaking contexts is your challenge. A group such as Toastmasters will help. Many organizations have their own club and most cities have several public clubs. Find a club you can join. You will find the investment of your time and the small club fees are well worth it. These clubs include both opportunities to practice prepared speeches and short impromptu answers to some fun questions. You will be able to wade into the water at your own pace. Best of all, the members will all want the same thing you do, to be more confident and articulate when speaking in front of others. Because they are working toward the same goal as you are, they can be the support you need and want as well as a tremendous source of helpful feedback.

Get expert help

There are a variety of experts you might seek out. A quick search on the internet will yield a plethora of consultants who will help you write better speeches, practice for interviews, control any distracting gestures or non-verbal behaviors, and/or guide you on posture and voice control. Rather than finding the right resource on your own, you might prefer to ask trusted sources for their recommendation.

The ideal resource to enlist is someone you know that has already mastered the skill you need. If, for example, you need to introduce a speaker at an event, you can ask someone who has made this kind of introduction many times before for guidance. They will have practical tips about what works for them and offer some insight regarding the unique challenges they have faced. I have a sister who has received a job offer from every interview she has ever attended. She would be a goldmine of advice for other job seekers. If you have attended a presentation in which the speaker was, in your estimation, particularly good, approach them a day or two later and ask if they would be willing to chat with you about how they planned their content and prepared for the delivery. It is a huge compliment to be asked for something like this and most people will respond with enthusiasm.

In addition to the in-person help you can get by approaching experts or hiring a coach, you can use books, videos, blogs, and podcasts for tips and guidance. The entire self-help industry is based on the premise that, given the right information, we can make advantageous changes in our behavior, attitudes, values, and beliefs. Unfortunately, however, just purchasing a book, reading an article, listening to something, or watching a video will not be very effective by itself. Passive access to self-help content will not help you toward your goal. You will have to practice and master the skills provided to get any benefit.

In addition to direct coaching on specific skills, you might consider some sessions with a certified hypnotherapist. They can help you develop more confidence and teach you to use tools that will de-escalate your stress response.

Whatever your need, there is someone who has the expertise to help you. In most cases you can probably handle addressing your needs on your own. You can do very well overcoming whatever obstacle gets in your way from being successful in high-stakes speaking situations. Sometimes, however, it is just easier, faster, or creates more confidence if you enlist the help of an expert.

Make some new friends

When I am speaking to an audience of any size, I try to arrive early. As people arrive, I chat with them about anything I can think of, such as the weather, traffic getting to the site, the venue, any current sporting event, why they chose to come to this event, etc. It doesn't matter what the topic is; I just try to make some connection with two or three people. I might even admit to them I am feeling a little tense. When I make that admission, they invariably smile and offer some encouragement because they can relate to that feeling. Then, when it comes time for me to speak, I now have a couple of friends in the audience. I look for them and make eye contact and once again, like co-conspirators, they respond with a smile. They want to help you, and that smile helps immensely.

Don't go it alone

You have choices. You don't have to do this alone. Other people feel the same way you do about high-stakes speaking situations. Reach out and you will discover a wealth of support waiting for you. Whether it's your family, friends, a social network such as Toastmasters, a coach, therapist, or a stranger you have just recruited to be your ally, you don't have to go it alone. Knowing there are people around you who want you to be successful and are helping you in whatever way they can, and it will make all the difference. There is safety in numbers, so make use of the numbers around you!

11
Reverse Engineering

"I got it! I got the job!" Brooke announced as she bounced up and down, waving a note pad.

"That's fantastic! You were so nervous about that interview. How did you manage it?" Clay asked.

"I used reverse engineering. Here it is, right here," Brooke explained as she placed her note pad in front of Clay.

Begin with the end in mind

Reverse engineering is one of Covey's ideas which was introduced in chapter seven. It is a concept that has been borrowed from the manufacturing industry and it involves taking an existing product and deconstructing it to learn how it was made or how it works. In this context, it refers to identifying exactly the outcome you want and being realistic about where you are right now in terms of your skills, priorities, and commitment to that outcome.

Once you are clear about your beginning and end point, you can do a 'brain-dump' of all the tasks you will need to complete to get from start to finish. It might be tempting to create a timeline and some tasks will lend themselves to such a timeline, but you will need to be flexible. Some tasks might need to be ongoing or repeated several times along your journey so don't get hung up on a specific order for the tasks. The value of reverse engineering is that it gives you a view of the landscape and ensures your continued awareness of the path you are on. With the complete plan in front of you, you can choose one thing to work on every day. If you do that, success is guaranteed.

Your checklist

The time to start building your confidence and learning to be calm when faced with a high-stakes speaking situation is now. Through practice today, when you are not being called upon to speak, you can be ready when you are called upon. Successful athletes know this. They spend an enormous number of hours preparing for their competitions by practicing a variety of exercises.

You can do this too. Here is a list of activities you can choose from. Work on mastering these tasks and you will see a big difference in your results. When you are asked to give a presentation, present a report, or attend a networking event, or an interview, or any other speaking situation in which your words will make a difference in people's perception of you, you will be able to think clearly and present your best self.

Every day for three weeks, review the list of exercises and activities. Choose one action to be your focus for the day. By changing your activity on a daily basis, you won't get bored. By doing something every day for three weeks, you will develop the habit of challenging your anxiety.

The checklist is available in the Appendix of this book. If you go to www.ICanspeakbook.com, you can print this checklist. It would be helpful to then post it near your desk to remind you of the many different tools you can use to help yourself.

I *Can* Speak Take-Action Checklist

- I will remind myself that being anxious about high-stakes speaking situations is normal and healthy. I will write the following statement on a post-it note: "My anxiety is my friend. It will push me to prepare myself properly for the event and increase my focus and concentration during the event. As a result, I will represent myself well." I will read the note to myself at least three times today.

- I will complete the *High-Stakes Speaking Scale* and compare my score to earlier scores. I will congratulate myself on my progress. If I do not see any progress or if I see an increase in my score, I will look at the items on the assessment and develop a plan to address those items.

- I will practice *beach ball breathing* or *alternating nostril breathing* three times today. I will set a timer for three minutes for each session or practice ten breaths for each session.

- I will review my self-affirmation statement and, if necessary, re-write it to better address my current situation. I might choose to write additional statements that I can use in the future.

- I will place my self-affirmation, "I am..." statements in at least three places where I will see them several times a day. Every time I see the statement, I will read it to myself or, if possible, read it out loud.

- I will set the alarm on my phone or watch for 60 minutes. Every time the alarm rings, I will check my posture and adjust it to take up more space, or I might choose to stand in a power-pose for one minute.

- I will set the alarm for seven minutes and use the hot pen method to answer the following question: "Feeling tense or anxious about speaking in a high-stakes situation is a good thing because…" I will then identify five keywords that inspire me. I will repeat these words to myself at least three times.

- I will listen to a self-hypnosis recording to bolster my confidence at least once today. This could be the recording available at www.ICanspeakbook.com, or I might use other self-hypnosis resources such as an app on my phone, a YouTube video, or an audio-book.

- I will set a timer for seven minutes and use the hot pen method to write a detailed description of how I will look and feel during my high-stakes speaking event. I will describe the outcome of that event. I will describe the outcome in terms of both my feelings and others' behaviors toward me. I will make this description thorough and positive. After writing the description, I will review it at least three times today.

- I will listen to a guided visualization recording from www.ICanSpeakbook.com or another source to help me see the positive outcome of my speaking event.

- I will identify my most problematic irrational beliefs using the assessment at
  http://www.testandcalc. com/Self_Defeating_Beliefs/

questtxt.asp. I will then write a dispute letter to myself and review it at least three times today.

- Each time I catch myself thinking negative thoughts about speaking in a high-stakes situation, I will practice the thought-stopping tool. With this tool, I will replace a negative thought with a more helpful positive thought.

- I will use gross motor movement for 30 minutes today. This will help me get more oxygen into my body and to think more clearly. I can do this through a series of short intervals that add up to 30 minutes, or I can do one 30-minute session.

- I will practice stretching exercises. I will do each of the four exercises described in chapter nine, or any other stretching exercise, at least three times a day.

- I will listen to the progressive relaxation recording available on www.ICanSpeak.com or a progressive relaxation recording from another resource at least once today.

- I will think of my audience as my ally, not the enemy. To do this, I will set a timer for seven minutes and use the hot pen method to explain to myself the ways in which my audience and I share the same purpose and why they want me to succeed.

- I will talk to my friends or family about the high-stakes speaking event and ask for their help in preparation.

- I will read a book, take a class, or watch a video that will help me manage anxiety or sharpen my speaking skills.

- I will find a local Toastmasters club and arrange to attend a meeting.

- I will create a plan for making new "friends" at a speaking event.

Getting control

It doesn't matter what you choose from the list. Practicing any one of these exercises will make a difference in your ability to show up and present your best self. The important point is that you practice every day for at least three weeks. Start this discipline before you need to. That means, *start now.* It is the consistent effort, not the specific exercises, that will make the difference for you.

The list gives you some great variety and addresses a range of issues associated with anxiety. With this list, you won't get bored and you will be better able to stay focused on getting the necessary practice. No excuses! You can do this! You can take back control of your emotions and feel calm and confident the next time you have to speak when the stakes are high.

12
The New You

Step into your future

How would things change for you if you could manage your emotions and be calm and confident in your high-stakes speaking opportunities? Achieving this isn't magic, it's preparation. The tools are available. You no longer have to be at the mercy of your stress response. You can summon your peak performance at will if you practice the tools. It's your choice.

Darcey's journey

Darcey's supervisor, Mavis, called me one day. She had a position posted and, when she checked with Human Resources, Darcey had not applied. Mavis was frustrated because the position would be a promotion for Darcey and if she applied, she would be the lead candidate. Mavis explained that Darcey was well suited for this new role and was well-respected in her department. She didn't understand why Darcey was not submitting her application and asked me to talk with Darcey.

When I met with Darcey, I asked her about the new role. This is how the conversation went.

Darcey said, "I know I can do most of the work. And believe me, my family could use the extra money that position would bring. I just can't bring myself to apply."

"Tell me what's getting in the way?" I probed.

"There are a few things. First, the thought of being interviewed makes my stomach sick. Second, I just can't see myself leading team meetings. I think I'll choke on my words and look like an idiot. Finally, part of that job is reporting progress to the steering committee and there is no way I can do that."

"Wow," I said. "That's a lot. I can see why you don't want to apply, but it sounds like you sort of do want the job. You said you believe you could do most of the work and you would really like the extra money, right?"

Darcey looked down and began rubbing her hand on the arm of the chair. "Yeah, but it isn't going to happen," she said in an almost whisper.

"What if it could?" I asked. "What if I could help you with the interview, leading a team meeting, and presenting to the steering committee? Would you be interested?"

She looked up, confused but with some hope in her eyes.

"I don't think that's possible. Is that something you can do? I've always been this way," she said.

"Are you interested in challenging your fears?" I asked pointedly. "It will take some work, but if you are willing, I believe you can do this."

Darcey's answer was a cautious yes, so we began immediately. If everything is important, then nothing is important. We needed to work on one issue at a time, and the obvious starting point was the job interview. I showed Darcey a list of actions she might take. That list was similar to the one provided to you in chapter eleven. After reviewing the list carefully and asking questions, she chose the following:

- To reframe her interviewers as her ally instead of her enemy.

  Darcey knew Mavis would be one of the interviewers and was also fairly sure of who Mavis would choose to assist her. I told her to use the hot pen method to explain to herself why Mavis would want her to be the successful candidate. How would she make Mavis' job easier?

When it was time to turn her attention to the other interviewer, Darcey smiled. She explained that it had to be one of two people, and, in the last year, she had completed important projects for each of the two. They had thanked her for the timeliness and the thoroughness of her work. I had Darcey add a paragraph to the hot pen assignment, explaining why either of these two potential interviewers would see Darcey as a good candidate for the promotion.

Once this assignment was completed, I instructed Darcey to read it to herself every night before she went to bed. That way, this message would be the last thing on her mind before she slept. This would give her subconscious an opportunity to integrate the message and act on it.

- To write a self-affirmation statement.

Using the guidelines described in chapter five, Darcey wrote a simple "I am..." self-affirmation statement. She then made it her screen saver on both her phone and her personal computer. By doing so, she would see this message several times a day and could then read it to herself each time.

- To listen to the self-hypnosis recording that dealt with confidence.

I reviewed with Darcey the many choices she had for selecting a good self-hypnosis recording and she chose to download the confidence self-hypnosis recording from www.ICanSpeakbook.com. We discussed when, in her daily routine, would be a good time to listen to the recording. She considered listening to the recording first thing in the morning but she quickly realized that she couldn't predict what time her little one would wake up, which might make it difficult to have a consistent time for herself. She decided that a good time would be at her desk on her lunch break. If she packed a lunch, which she recognized would save a few dollars and might even be a healthier choice than regularly eating out, there would be time for both enjoying the recording and eating her lunch.

We agreed that Darcey would work on these three activities for one week, and we would then get together. In the meantime, she was to submit her application for the job. She could always withdraw the application if she didn't feel ready, so there was really no risk in filling it out. Darcey agreed and headed back to her job.

When we met the second time, I explained that, since her interview was scheduled for the next week, it was time to put a couple of the other actions into effect:

- Anxiety is your friend. It will push you to do the work to properly prepare for your high-stakes speaking event, which in this case, was Darcey's interview.

I asked Darcey if it would help to think about what questions might be asked by the interviewers. That way she could think about her answers in advance of the interview. She readily agreed so we began writing generic questions that many interviewers use. We searched the internet for more good questions and added them to our list.

Now came the more difficult step: it was time to consider some job-specific questions Mavis and her interview partner might ask. At first, Darcey felt stumped by this task but when I suggested we review the job description, it was not difficult to identify five potential task-specific questions.

- Getting help from family and friends.

With the list of potential interview questions, we practiced the interview. I would ask a question, and Darcey would answer. I would then give her feedback on her answer, and if she needed to adjust it, we would practice the new answer. When we had worked through the lengthy list of questions, I told Darcey to continue this practice with a family member. Darcey said she knew her sister would help, and she would call her tonight to schedule some practice sessions.

Before we finished our session, I explained to Darcey there was one more thing she needed to do.

- Use the power pose.

  I asked Darcey to stand up and to place her hands on her hips. With her chin up, her chest out, and her feet shoulder length apart, I asked her to repeat her self-affirmation "I am..." statement. I had her repeat the statement twice more, louder each time. I then suggested that she go to the restroom ten minutes before the interview and repeat this exercise.

As we concluded the session, I asked Darcey how she felt about attending the interview. She admitted she still felt anxious, but it wasn't overwhelming.

"Are you going to withdraw your application?" I asked.

"No, I know I can manage the interview now. I'm still pretty anxious about the team meetings and reporting sessions, though. When can we start on that?" she responded.

We scheduled another session for the day after her interview. When we met, Darcey hadn't heard yet whether she got the job or not but that didn't change our focus. Once again, I asked Darcey which three things on the action checklist she would like to choose to practice for the next seven days. She could have chosen any of the exercises she had already practiced but she wanted to experience more on the list, so she chose the following:

- To identify five key words to inspire her.

To do that she would use the hot pen method to complete the following statement: "Feeling tense or anxious about speaking in a high-stakes situation is a good thing because…" After reviewing what she had written, she would look for the five words that stood out.

- To practice Beach Ball Breathing three times a day.

While practicing her breathing, as she exhaled, Darcey would repeat one of the five keywords three times. On the next breath, she would repeat a different keyword on her exhale. After working through all five keywords, she would repeat the entire sequence for a total of ten breaths.

- To use thought-stopping when she had a negative thought about leading her team.

Darcey suggested that she wear a rubber band around a wrist. As she would tell herself to stop a negative thought and replace it with a positive thought, she would move the rubber band to her other wrist. This physical action would serve to further distract her negative thinking as she focused on moving the rubber band.

After discussing these ideas, Darcy enthusiastically said, "I'm going to keep doing all the things we practiced last week, plus these new actions."

"That sounds great on the surface, Darcey," I commented. "But I'm concerned about you being overwhelmed and then giving up. Remember, if everything is important then nothing is important. You will be more successful if you focus your efforts. It's not like you can't practice those items once in a while, but don't put pressure on yourself to do them every day."

Darcey nodded her head in agreement, and we ended our session by rescheduling our next meeting for the following week.

The week was a busy one and before I knew it, Darcey was back in my office.

"I got the job!" Darcey announced.

"How are you feeling about that?" I asked.

"I am really excited," she said. "I thought I would be nervous, but I think I can do it now. I'm going to need to continue to practice the exercises you taught me, but

I don't get sick to my stomach when I think of leading my team or even reporting to the senior team."

"That's great, Darcey, but we haven't worked on that third issue, reporting. Do you still want to do that?" I asked.

"It doesn't feel like such a big deal now," she said confidently. "The more I practice the exercises, the less anxious I feel about anything. The other day the Vice President of our division stopped me in the hall to congratulate me on my promotion. Ordinarily my heart would have been pounding and I wouldn't have been able to talk. Instead, I just took a deep breath, smiled and thanked her. I know it doesn't sound like a lot, but I can't believe it, I didn't feel like I was going to faint."

"That isn't surprising to me, when you make progress on taking back control of one fear, it generalizes to others. You have skills now and it makes a significant difference," I responded. "So, are we done?"

Darcey smiled as she said, "I think so!"

I smiled back and sat up in my chair. "Okay but I want to finish with a couple of reminders."

I raised my index finger to indicate number one, "Use your anxiety to work for you and prepare for your reporting sessions. Take a few minutes to anticipate what concerns the senior team might have and what questions they might ask you about your report. That way you can write your answers down and put them in a folder. Just having the folder with you will help you to feel more comfortable."

Raising another finger, I said, "Second, take a few minutes to beach ball breathe and make sure your posture is open and strong. Use the power pose if you want."

Using a third finger to indicate my final point, I continued, "Finally, you might re-take the High-Stakes Speaking Scale assessment. I believe you are going to see a significant difference. When you take it, print the initial and current scores to remind yourself of how far you have come."

With that, we both stood and Darcey surprised me with a quick hug. I checked in with Darcey's supervisor, Mavis, a year later. Mavis told me that Darcey has blossomed into a confident and respected leader in her area. Her team was the most productive in the department and Darcey had become the "go-to" person her colleagues went to for help. When I talked with Darcey, she admitted she still had a few butterflies when she had to talk to the senior team, but they were becoming less and less frequent and intense. Much to her surprise, she no longer dreaded leading her own team meetings. She actually looked forward to them now.

Your journey

Darcey has come a long, long way. Not only is her career progressing, but she is also truly enjoying the sense of control she has achieved over her own emotions. Without tackling her fears, she would still be in her original position, under-performing given her potential. Her journey can be yours. I chose Darcey's story because her fears had generalized across several speaking contexts. If left alone, they would have generalized or deepened because that is what fear does. If you allow fear to exist in one context, it always spills into other, related areas. You don't have to accept living with fear. You can take back control.

You deserve better than the way you are treating yourself. Imagine what your career and your life might look like if you were more comfortable speaking in situations in which all eyes are on you. You would think more clearly, respond more articulately and, without question, feel better about yourself.

My promise to you is that, if you use the checklist from the previous chapter to select actions that feel right for you, your anxiety about speaking in high-stakes situations will dramatically ease. You don't have to take my word for it. In fact, please don't simply take my word for it! Test it for yourself. After working with your choice of tools for a few weeks, re-test yourself using the High-Stakes Speaking Scale.

I would love to hear from you about your success. Send me an email and let me know the difference you've made!

References

Brown, Brené (2007). *I Thought It Was Just Me (But It Isn't): Making the journey from "What will people think?" to "I am enough."* NY: Avery.

Covey, Stephen (1994). *The Seven Habits of Highly Effective People: Powerful lessons in personal change.* DC Books.

Cuddy, Amy (2018). *Presence: Bringing your bolder self to your biggest challenges.* Boston, MA: Little, Brown Spark. Ellis, Albert, Harper, Robert A., and Powers, Melvin (1975). *A Guide to Rational Living.* 3rd Ed. Woodland Hills, CA: Wilshire Book Company.

Nongard, Richard (2018). *Reframing Hypnotherapy: Evidence-based techniques for your next hypnosis session.* Scottsdale, AZ: Nongard.

Selye, Hans (1974). *Stress without Distress: How to Survive in a Stressful Society.* Baltimore, MD: Lippincott Williams & Wilkins.

Stanhope, B. (2018). *The Golden Sayings of Epictetus: In contemporary English with explanatory notes.* Stanhope Publishing.

Appendix A

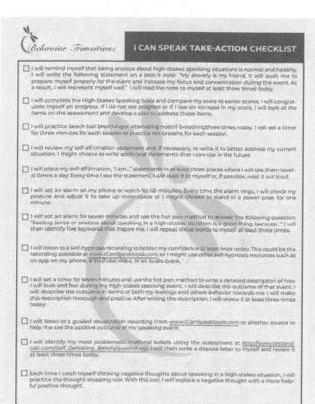

Behavior Transitions — I CAN SPEAK TAKE-ACTION CHECKLIST

☐ I will use gross motor movement for thirty minutes today. This will help me get more oxygen into my body and to think more clearly. I can do this through a series of short intervals that add up to thirty minutes or I can do one thirty-minute session.

☐ I will practice stretching exercises. I will do each of the four exercises described in chapter nine, or any other stretching exercise, at least three times a day.

☐ I will listen to the progressive relaxation recording available on www.ICanSpeak.com or a progressive relaxation recording from another resource at least once today.

☐ I will think of my audience as my ally, not the enemy. To do this, I will set a timer for seven minutes and use the hot pen method to explain to myself the ways in which my audience and I share the same purpose and why they want me to succeed.

☐ I will talk to my friends or family about the high-stakes speaking event and ask for their help in preparation.

☐ I will read a book, take a class, or watch a video that will help me manage anxiety or sharpen my speaking skills.

☐ I will find a local Toastmasters club and arrange to attend a meeting.

☐ I will create a plan for making new "friends" at a speaking event.

If you would like personal coaching, you can contact me at: **DrPaula@behaviortransitions.com** or visit my website at **www.BehaviorTransitions.com**

Notes:

②

Other Books by
Dr. M. Paula Daoust

Most people are not good at a skill that is critical to their job! Even when they attend training, their skill does not improve. Why? Because conflict is an emotional experience and not a rational, logical event.

If your goal is to get better outcomes when dealing with conflict and you are like most people, you probably need some help in learning to manage your emotions. This book is packed full of tools that you can use today to make a difference in your career. Like a buffet, you can pick and choose the tools that feel most comfortable for you or will fit best with your situation. When you put together a plan that feels right for you, you will get those better outcomes you need and want.

117

Coming Soon!

Are you excelling in your sales performance or just getting by? There are lots of great books that teach effective sales techniques. But if you want to rise above the average, you need more than techniques - you need to use your whole brain: your logical, analytic brain and your emotional brain. The sales frontier has changed, but one thing is still the same, people buy with their emotions.

By using a variety of tools that are based on the latest brain science, you will learn to tap into the power of your whole mind. With these tools, you can breakthrough to exceptional sales success.

You are invited!

Dr. M. Paula Daoust offers workshops for groups in either the traditional classroom format or via Zoom. Workshops are available for either speaking in high-stakes speaking situations or resolving conflict. In addition, workshops can be tailored to your group's specific needs.

As a professional instructional designer, Dr. M. Paula Daoust will provide your group with an engaging, highly interactive experience that will get results!

Learn from the expert that can guide you and your group to the results you need and want!

Email DrPaula@behaviortransitions.com for more information!